The Nonprofit Marketing Guide

SECOND EDITION

The Nonprofit Marketing Guide

High-Impact, Low-Cost Ways to
Build Support for Your Good Cause

KIVI LEROUX MILLER

WILEY

For general information on our other products and services or for technical support, please contact our Customer Care Department within the United States at (800) 762-2974, outside the United States at (317) 572-3993 or fax (317) 572-4002.

Wiley publishes in a variety of print and electronic formats and by print-on-demand. Some material included with standard print versions of this book may not be included in e-books or in print-on-demand. If this book refers to media such as a CD or DVD that is not included in the version you purchased, you may download this material at http://booksupport.wiley.com. For more information about Wiley products, visit www.wiley.com.

Library of Congress Cataloging-in-Publication Data is available:

ISBN 9781119771036 (Paperback)
ISBN 9781119771050 (ePDF)
ISBN 9781119771043 (ePub)

Cover Design: Wiley
Cover Image: © Sungjin Kim/Getty Images
Author Photo: Courtesy of the Author

SKY10025039_021721

For Edgar, Ava, and Jianna, the pot of gold at the end of my rainbow.

CONTENTS

CHAPTER SEVENTEEN Find the Time: Get More Done
in Fewer Hours **207**

CHAPTER EIGHTEEN Conclusion: How Do You Know
Whether You Are Doing a Good Job? **215**

PREFACE: THE STORY BEHIND THIS BOOK

When I wrote the first edition of this book in 2010, it came largely from my personal experience. I started consulting as a freelance writer for nonprofits in 1998, after nearly a decade of working for nonprofits as a staff member, dedicated board member, and volunteer.

My freelance writing career was quickly revolutionized like everything else by the exponential growth of the Internet. Soon I was learning HTML and Photoshop, and then creating marketing strategies, drafting communications budgets, and attempting to calculate return-on-investment for all of this work that was, in so many ways, brand-new to the nonprofit sector.

The job of the modern nonprofit communications director was born, and I was one of the people trying to fill this new role for several different nonprofit clients. Throughout that decade from 2000 to 2010, I learned how to be that nonprofit marketing department of one. I experimented all the time, producing both successes and failures, but always learning.

I didn't, however, have any kind of roadmap for this work. It just didn't exist because the job was evolving just as fast as the Internet. I vowed that at some point I would write it myself.

At the same time, I began teaching workshops, first through the Social Action and Leadership School for Activists (SALSA) program in Washington, D.C., and then through Duke University's certificate program in nonprofit management in North Carolina. Because I enjoyed teaching so much, in 2007 I transitioned my business from primarily consulting to primarily training. I launched NonprofitMarketingGuide.com, including a blog and weekly webinar series.

My hunch that staff at thousands of nonprofits were in the exact same situation that my clients and I had been in for many years was right: they too were communications departments of just one or two people who had to do it all themselves and didn't know where to turn for help. The response to Nonprofit Marketing Guide the company was so positive that I knew it was time to write an eponymous book, which was published in 2010.

The nonprofit communications profession has continued to evolve in leaps and bounds since then. I was pleasantly surprised to see many college and university certificate and degree programs begin teaching about marketing in the nonprofit sector, assigning this book as required reading. I was especially tickled one day in 2016 when one of my best friends from high school posted a photo of her daughter's college textbook on Facebook – and it was this book!

Throughout 2010–2020, I too was studying nonprofit communications and marketing in earnest. At Nonprofit Marketing Guide, we launched an annual *Nonprofit Communications Trends Report* sharing the results of survey data from thousands of nonprofits. We also launched a number of training, coaching, and mentoring programs for nonprofit communications staff that allowed me to see the inner workings of hundreds of nonprofits. Over the years, we studied not only the communications tactics nonprofits use, but how the required skill set is changing, the challenges staff in the job face each day, and what communications effectiveness looks like in the nonprofit sector.

I shared what we continued to learn in two additional books, the award-winning *Content Marketing for Nonprofit: A Communications Map for Engaging Your Community, Becoming a Favorite Cause, and Raising More Money* (Jossey-Bass, 2013) and *CALM not BUSY: How to Manage Your Nonprofit's Communications for Great Results* (Bold & Bright Media, 2018).

I think of those books as the 201 and 301 texts for nonprofit communicators. As 2020 and another new decade approached, I knew it was time to revisit the 101 book. I've updated *The Nonprofit Marketing Guide* for a new generation of communications professionals and career changers getting started in the sector.

While these new members of our profession are on my mind as I write and edit this edition, I am also surrounded in spirit by literally thousands of generous souls who have helped me learn every lesson that I am sharing in this book. It is truly a collective effort, and for each and every interaction and conversation that culminated into the thinking and experiences shared on these pages, I am eternally grateful.

Kivi Leroux Miller
September 2020

INTRODUCTION: HOW TO USE THIS BOOK

This book is meant to be part real-world survival guide and part nitty-gritty how-to handbook for busy nonprofit marketers with small budgets and staff, including executive directors who are asked to do it all, and anyone new to the work of nonprofit marketing and communications. I hope it is both a reference that you'll return to often and a comforting support, reassuring you that you really can do this, even if you are working on your own. Crease up the spine, mark up the pages, and make it your own personal guide to marketing your good cause.

The book is organized into four sections.

Part One: Getting Ready to Do It Right gives you some big-picture perspective on the world of nonprofit marketing and provides context for everything else that follows in the book. It includes chapters on planning, effectiveness, listening, and more.

Part Two: Answering the Three Most Important Nonprofit Marketing Questions dives into defining your target communities, creating messaging that works, and delivering those messages in the best ways.

Part Three: Building a Community of Supporters Around You recognizes the profound shift in how people and nonprofits are connecting with and relating to each other and will help you build your own community of supporters.

Part Four: Doing It Yourself Without Doing Yourself In looks at the trio of elements required for successful implementation of any marketing program: time, talent, and treasure.

The book concludes with some suggestions for the big questions to ask yourself as you evaluate the success of your nonprofit marketing program.

You can approach the book in the way that works best for you: read it straight through, or backward, or start in the middle. The detailed table of contents in the front, as well as an index in the back, can help you quickly find the sections you need.

LOOKING FOR MORE?

To continue the learning and conversation, we invite you to join us at NonprofitMarketingGuide.com and to follow us on social media. Look for @npmktgd and @kivilm. You will also find a companion workbook to help you implement what you learn in the book at npmg.us/workbook.

PART ONE

Getting Ready to Do It Right

Nonprofit marketing is hard work. It's also tremendously fun and satisfying, especially when you do it right. Your work will challenge you in ways you have yet to understand, and you'll learn about disciplines that you had never considered before. Because nonprofit marketing is complex, it can quickly overwhelm people new to the field. This is particularly true if it's something thrown on top of your "real" job as an executive director, development director, or program manager. This book should make your job a little easier.

In Chapter 1, I review 10 realities of marketing and communications work that are the foundation for the thinking in the rest of the book. Chapter 2 defines nonprofit marketing and the many choices you have for marketing goals, strategies, objectives, and tactics as a nonprofit communicator. Chapter 3 gives you an overview of what a full-blown marketing strategy looks like, what tactical communications plans include, and how to do a quick-and-dirty version if that is all you can handle.

Chapter 4 outlines the different stages or levels of effectiveness that nonprofits move through as their communications staff become more skilled and their organizations fully embrace marketing best practices. The final chapter in this section, Chapter 5, explains why listening (call it market research if you prefer) is essential to any successful nonprofit marketing strategy and how you can use a variety of tools and methods to learn a great deal about the people you are working with and serving.

10 Realities of Nonprofit Marketing

I opened the first edition of this book with a chapter called "10 New Realities for Nonprofits" with an emphasis on "New." Back in 2010, I was still urging nonprofits to be OK with calling this work "marketing" rather than euphemisms like "outreach," to take social media seriously, and to convince them that people over 50 really were using the Internet. Thankfully, we've moved well beyond those sticking points.

All of the other elements in that original list proved foundational to the work of nonprofit communications. While I have updated this list, what you'll find here are the assumptions on which all of the other chapters in the book are built. Understanding this list will help you get the most out of this book and to understand the choices I suggest you make.

Many forces beyond your control will affect how you market your nonprofit organization. The economy will go up and down. Friendly elected officials will be in charge, and then they will lose an election. Talented volunteers, staff, and board members will come and go. What people can do from their phones no matter where they are in the world will continue to grow.

But I don't expect the following 10 realities to change much.

REALITY 1: MARKETING EFFECTIVENESS DEPENDS ON A CONFIDENT, SKILLED PROFESSIONAL

At Nonprofit Marketing Guide, we've been researching communication effectiveness at nonprofits for more than a decade. I can tell you with absolute confidence that nonprofits that treat marketing and communications like the specialty profession that it is get better results.

Each of us communicates every day, and as a result, many of us think we are good writers, have good taste and a sense of style, and assume that others like the same things we do. Unfortunately, it's just not true! Successfully marketing a nonprofit organization requires an overly broad set of skills to be applied to a relatively narrow set of priorities. As the work becomes more and more dependent on sophisticated technology, it's even more important to employ staff who understand what they are doing and are committed to their own ongoing professional development.

REALITY 2: MARKETING EFFECTIVENESS DEPENDS ON A SUPPORTIVE ORGANIZATIONAL CULTURE

For maximum effectiveness, your confident and skilled marketing staff need to work within an organizational culture that values marketing and communications.

Too often nonprofits just want communications staff to make all the stuff – the social media and website updates, the newsletters, flyers, and event invitations, etc. The least effective organizations treat their communications staff like fast-food drive-through windows, taking orders and churning out content.

In contrast, supportive organizations understand that you need more than just communications tactics for success. You need real strategy. You need planning. You need adequate resources, including time, talent, and treasure. You need to view marketing and communications as an essential, valued function.

REALITY 3: THERE WILL ALWAYS BE TOO MUCH TO DO

Nonprofit marketing work comes with an overabundance of options and decisions to make. You simply cannot do it all. You have to make choices, and that can be incredibly challenging to do.

Communications staff who don't understand this and don't learn to manage expectations for both themselves and their organizations will find themselves burned out within a few years. I never expected to incorporate the concept of setting personal boundaries into my communications coaching practice, but it's become an essential skill.

REALITY 4: THERE IS NO SUCH THING AS THE GENERAL PUBLIC

When I teach nonprofit marketing workshops, I often make participants chant this with me in unison, so they remember it: "There is no such thing as the general public! There is no such thing as the general public!"

The general public includes *everyone*, from newborns to elders, from rich to poor, from incarcerated to the jet set. No matter how much you try, you will not reach everyone. In fact, if that's what you try to do, odds are good that you will reach no one. Instead, you need to focus on specific groups of people and work toward communicating with them in ways that connect with their particular needs and values.

When nonprofit marketing programs fail, organizations too frequently blame the tactics. "We tried an email newsletter, but no one read it." "We sent out a direct mail fundraising letter, but it didn't raise much money." Closer examination of those tactics often reveals that the message was too generic and therefore spoke to no one in particular.

All communications should be created with particular groups of people in mind. That's the only way to create content that people will find relevant.

REALITY 5: YOU NEED TO MANAGE YOUR OWN MEDIA EMPIRE

The multitude of ways to communicate directly with the world has never been more accessible, largely built on the evolution of both social media and mobile technology.

I encourage all nonprofits to think of themselves as media moguls. At a minimum, you are likely managing a website, email, and a couple of social media channels. Most nonprofits go far beyond this list to include print mailing, media relations, in-person and online events, and more.

Do not think of all of these different ways to communicate (we call them "channels") as separate and independent from each other. At a minimum, use a multichannel approach where you think through how to share your content across several different channels. Your community can interact with you in each channel.

Even better, take an omnichannel approach where you deliver your content across many channels in a way that creates a more consistent, seamless experience for your community. Where a multichannel approach centers on how your messaging appears in different places, an omnichannel approach centers on how your community members experience your messaging, regardless of channel.

REALITY 6: NONPROFIT MARKETING IS A FORM OF COMMUNITY ORGANIZING

Although you'll be encouraged in this book to remember that your supporters are real, individual people and to speak to them personally, it's also important to remember the power of your network as a whole and the connections that your supporters have with each other.

Think about when you host events. Isn't it wonderful to see all of those people who care about your work in one place, talking to each other about the good work you are doing, and feeling good about their contributions to something much bigger than themselves?

Smart nonprofit marketers find those people who are enthusiastic about the cause and who also have large networks of their own. You then feed those big fans and help them spread the message to others. They may fundraise for you, but just as important, they also "friendraise" for you.

Consider integrating fundraising, marketing, communications, and information technology into community building or community engagement teams. Incorporate all that is learned through your community of supporters into program design and implementation. Using marketing to facilitate community building is likely the best way to achieve your nonprofit's ultimate mission.

REALITY 7: PERSONAL AND ORGANIZATIONAL BRANDS OFTEN BLEND

What emotions does your nonprofit evoke in people? What is your group known for? This is your organization's brand, image, or personality – and many nonprofits are finding that their organizational brand is closely related to the personalities of their most public staff members. This has always been true for smaller organizations, groups led by a founding or longtime executive director, and nonprofits created in someone else's memory or honor.

But now larger nonprofits must contend with this reality too. Good online marketing, especially in social media, is personal, which means that your staff should present themselves as real human beings in your communications. This mixing of personal and professional can be quite uncomfortable for people who highly value their privacy or who hold on to more traditional or dated definitions of what is professional and what is not.

The personality of the messenger – you – can affect the message. Think about your own personality and voice – your personal brand – and how it impacts the organization's brand.

REALITY 8: GOOD NONPROFIT MARKETING TAKES MORE TIME THAN MONEY

Because the Internet has revolutionized communications between organizations and individuals, effective nonprofit marketing programs can be implemented for online pennies on the print dollar. Although you still need a budget to pay for good web hosting; email service providers; some upgraded, professional-level services; and, of course, staff, lack of money is no longer the biggest stumbling block to good nonprofit marketing. Now the sticking point is lack of time.

Engaging supporters in conversations is more time-consuming than blasting messages out to them. Managing profiles on multiple social media sites is more time-consuming than updating your website once a month. Writing a blog with several posts per week is more time-consuming than sending out a print newsletter twice a year. Although all of these tasks do take more time, they are also more effective at building a community of supporters and encouraging them to act on your behalf.

REALITY 9: YOU'VE ALREADY LOST CONTROL OF YOUR MESSAGE – STOP PRETENDING OTHERWISE

One of the most frequent concerns we used to hear from nonprofits about using social media and participating in conversations with people online was that they would lose control of their messages. They feared people would say bad things or manipulate their image in some way.

It's questionable whether that kind of control really ever existed, but the reality is that it is long gone. If someone wants to bad-mouth you online, they can do it right now whether you are there to see it and respond or not. Shutting down your computer or phone won't prevent those conversations from happening. They'll just happen without you there to correct any misconceptions.

Rather than trying to avoid awkward, negative, or challenging conversations online, your better approach is to learn ways to effectively engage in and, where possible, manage the way those conversations play out over time. Try to bring consistency to your messaging. It's much easier to steer a conversation and to suggest topics for additional discussion than it is to control what people say.

REALITY 10: MARKETING IS NOT FUNDRAISING, BUT IT IS ESSENTIAL TO IT

Good nonprofit marketing has many possible outcomes, and raising dollars is one of them. But nonprofits also use marketing to find and galvanize volunteers; to persuade decision makers; to change public policy; to raise awareness; to encourage behavior changes; to converse with clients, supporters, and partners; to foment social change – and more.

Although you can have successful long-term marketing campaigns that don't involve fundraising, you cannot have successful long-term fundraising campaigns without marketing. Marketing and communications are how you talk to your donors in between those times when you ask for money. They're what pull new people into your pool of potential new donors and what keep current donors happy with your organization so they will give again.

This is not a fundraising guide, but you'll find fundraising-related tips and examples throughout the book, because that is one result of successful nonprofit marketing.

CONCLUSION: TRY BOLDLY, AND TRY AGAIN

There is no one best way to market your nonprofit or your good cause, although some approaches have better odds of working than others, especially given these ten realities. I've tried to include in this book both the strategies and tactics that I believe will have the greatest likelihood of success, especially for smaller organizations, but you won't know what works best for your group and your supporters until you try, gauge the results, and try again.

Don't fear failure in your nonprofit marketing. Fear will make your approaches too conservative, and you'll become just another one of the thousands of really good causes out there that struggle day to day because they don't get the support they deserve.

Instead, be bold. Author and pastor Basil King said, "Be bold and mighty forces will come to your aid." You won't get it right the first time, and maybe not the second either. What's important is that you try new ways to reach out and grab hold of your supporters' hearts and minds. When you do, they will come to your aid.

chapter TWO

Defining Marketing in the Nonprofit Sector

When Jane Austin, the marketing director for AchieveMpls, which runs career and college readiness initiatives for high school students in Minneapolis and Saint Paul, started her job several years ago, the communications work was scattered across the organization. "Things were . . . a mess," said Jane. "The website was broken. Our mission statement didn't match our actual work. No one could describe what we did. New program videos, social media accounts, and taglines popped up without notice. Our red logo appeared in a wide range of shades from pink to orange. Our designers and web consultants were far too expensive."

Jane knew she had her work cut out for her. Getting communications on track and into the care of a professional team felt overwhelming. The other staff were long accustomed to managing their own communications projects and were suspicious of Jane's questions and offers of help.

She started with some baby steps. "Most importantly, I started by learning about my new colleagues and building their trust. I took the view that my colleagues were my clients, and I met with them to find out about their needs. I worked hard to be an attentive and responsive listener, sharing my vision that we were partners in our marketing work," said Jane.

Over time, communications projects and decision making began to shift to Jane as she demonstrated that she knew what she was doing and could produce good work on schedule and below cost. Jane began creating new office systems, assembling a team to help build a new website, reaching out to media, and securing new vendors. As trust in Jane grew, she was able to create new communications guidelines and protocols to guide AchieveMpls's communications work and create more consistency across the organization.

"Now several years later, our little marketing team is seen as an integral partner in our programmatic and community outreach work," said Jane. "We work hard to keep innovating our marketing work and also pay close attention to the importance of internal communications in building staff engagement." As a result, Jane has seen AchieveMpls's visibility and reputation in the community grow, while finding her team playing an increasingly important leadership role in the health and vitality of her organization.

At Nonprofit Marketing Guide, we meet many communications staff who are at the beginning of Jane's journey: in the middle of a hot mess. Much of the work we do is centered on helping people like her do exactly what she did: professionalize the marketing and communications functions within her organization.

It's rarely an easy journey, and it often takes several years, as is it did for Jane.

Many nonprofit leaders, especially those who come to their organizations because of a passionate commitment to a specific cause, mistakenly believe that nonprofit marketing is about nothing more than creating newsletters and social media updates about the good work the nonprofit is doing. Those with corporate experience sometimes narrowly define nonprofit marketing as brand management, public relations, and advertising. Still others, especially those responsible for fundraising, believe that all nonprofit marketing should direct people to donate money. While their numbers have certainly dwindled since the first edition of this book, some people still believe that marketing is nothing more than self-interested selling that has no place in the nonprofit sector. (Those people are, of course, wrong.)

In fact, marketing in the nonprofit sector is much, much more than any of these incomplete assumptions. To manage it effectively, it's vital to understand the depth and breadth of the work.

In this chapter, we'll review a more complete definition of marketing and how it applies to the nonprofit world. We'll also look at the difference between *marketing* and *communications*. Then we'll get even more specific by reviewing and defining the most common nonprofit marketing goals, strategies, objectives, and tactics.

THE OFFICIAL DEFINITION OF MARKETING

Consider this official definition of marketing from the American Marketing Association: "Marketing is the activity, set of institutions, and processes for creating, communicating, delivering, and exchanging offerings that have value for customers, clients, partners, and society at large."

As you can see, it's much more than just *communicating* about the programs or services that your nonprofit provides. Marketing is also about *creating* those programs or services, from the outset, and *delivering* them to your participants and supporters. Thus, marketing is not just something you do when you have the time or money; it's an essential component of a well-run organization, right alongside strategic planning, financial management, and evaluation of your effectiveness in implementing your mission.

Also included in the formal definition of marketing is *exchanging offerings that have value* – in simpler terms, you give a valuable to someone and you get one from them in return. In the business world, a person gives money to a business and the business gives them a service or product, like a box of cereal. But long before you walk out of the grocery store with a box of Crunchy Cocoa Flakes, the business's marketing department has helped determine how that cereal tastes and what it looks like in the bowl, because they have learned all about the cereal preferences of people that make up families like yours. They've figured out how much to charge you for it, based not on production costs alone but also on what they think you'd be willing to pay. They've also decided which stores will carry the cereal on their shelves. They've figured out what the box should look like and what they need to put in the TV commercials, so your kids won't stop bugging you until you add Crunchy Cocoa Flakes to the shopping list.

Of course, it's not quite that simple in the nonprofit world.

Instead of boxes of cereal, nonprofits are often "selling" products and services that are much more abstract, such as education, advocacy, facilitation, technical assistance, and networking. Many times, the characteristics and descriptions of those products and services are not solely for the nonprofit to decide; they are defined instead by government agencies, foundations, and other institutions that fund or regulate the nonprofit's programs.

The exchange is also not as simple as swiping a debit card and walking out of a store with a bag full of groceries. In the nonprofit world, programs are often offered to individuals for free, because their creation is paid for by contracts, grants, or charitable donations. The individual participants pay for what's offered with something other than money, such as their time, by performing a desired action, or simply by demonstrating a willingness to consider a different point of view.

In addition to these costs to both the nonprofit and the participants, we must also consider what's called the "benefit exchange." What does the nonprofit get out of it, and what does the participant get out of it? Where is the real value to both parties? Nonprofits often get one step closer to achieving their mission, whether it's reducing domestic violence or beautifying a neighborhood. Participants, on the other hand, often get some kind of emotional payback, such as feeling physically safer or knowing they've made their community a better place for their children.

The same is true for people who support nonprofits with donations of time, talent, and money. Nonprofits receive these benefits and in exchange, supporters get something too. Sometimes it's concrete, like tickets to an event or a fancy meal. Other times, it's an emotional benefit, such as feeling proud or inspired. Supporting a nonprofit can also affirm one's identity as a good person or as someone who makes a difference in the lives of others.

IS THIS WORK CALLED *MARKETING* OR *COMMUNICATIONS* OR SOMETHING ELSE?

I participate in numerous social media groups for nonprofit communicators, and several times a year, someone wants to debate the difference between *marketing* and *communications*. Sometimes words like *public relations* or *outreach* are also thrown in the mix. Many of these debates center on which words should be included in someone's job title or team name. As organizations grow, we also sometimes see battles about which executives or staff teams will control the various aspects of marketing and communications work, which also leads to parsing the definitions as the work is divided.

The practical reality is that both words, *marketing* and *communications*, are used interchangeably in the nonprofit sector. *Communications* director, manager, or coordinator is a much more common job title than *marketing* director, manager, or coordinator. However, those communications directors are almost always doing what I consider both marketing and communications work.

When asked to define the differences between *marketing* and *communications*, I tend to simplify the conversation by saying that marketing is the more strategic form of this work, and communications is the more tactical form.

Marketing is about the value exchange. You have to know who you are talking to, what messages will resonate with them, and the best ways to deliver those messages. Those are strategic choices. Communications, on the other hand, is all of the content you create and your plan to distribute that content so that you can maintain relationships with the people consuming that content. Every nonprofit needs both.

Again, in practice, both words are used interchangeably in the nonprofit sector. If you are speaking with someone who insists the terms are different, I encourage you to explore their definitions in the context of your conversation, so you fully understand the implications of those word choices.

A MORE MEANINGFUL DISTINCTION: MARKETING FOR FUNDRAISING OR FOR COMMUNITY ENGAGEMENT

After coaching hundreds of nonprofit communications directors, I've found that rather than debating whether they are doing marketing or communications, it's more meaningful to discuss whether they are marketing for the primary purpose of fundraising or marketing for the much broader purpose of community engagement.

Through the many years of research for Nonprofit Marketing Guide's annual *Nonprofit Communications Trends Reports*, we found a pattern: communications directors answered our survey questions quite differently depending on the "why" behind their work. We found a nearly equal split: about half of nonprofit communicators work directly in support of fundraising goals and the other half work more broadly for community engagement, which may or may not include some fundraising.

Communications staff who work primarily in service of fundraising goals have a more well-defined target audience: donors. Much of the communications they produce fit within the "Ask, Thank, Report" donor communications cycle. They ask for donations, then thank donors for their support – both individually and collectively – and then report back on the good works that those donors have made possible, often using a supporter-centered style of writing. (We'll explore ways to express gratitude in particular in Chapter 9 and various nonprofit writing styles in Chapter 10.) These communicators often focus more on direct mail and events as communications channels, as compared with staff who are not personally responsible for fundraising goals.

The other half of nonprofit communicators focus more broadly on community engagement, with fundraising as a secondary or tertiary goal, if at all. Their primary goals, target audiences, messages, and communications channels are usually much more varied than those of communicators focused more narrowly on fundraising.

But what does *community engagement* mean? Just as with the conversation about the difference between *marketing* and *communications*, it's essential that you define what community engagement means in the specific context of your work, because it can mean many different things.

At Nonprofit Marketing Guide, we define *community engagement* simply as keeping people inspired by and active in the work. To elaborate, community engagement includes *awareness, interaction*, and *participation*. Let's look at these elements a bit closer.

Awareness

Awareness is about introducing your organization and/or your issues to people for the first time. Communications activities like search engine optimization, media relations, and list building are common awareness activities.

Interaction

Interaction is about getting people to demonstrate that they are willing to move beyond just being aware of you and your cause. Activities such as liking, commenting, and sharing on social media are forms of interaction. Opening emails and clicking on links, downloading documents, and other simple form completions on your website would also fall under interaction.

Participation

Participation is a form of engagement that requires following through on a call to action of some sort. It could result in learning more, advocating for your cause, attending an event, donating, or volunteering.

As you think about what community engagement really means for your organization, give these three categories some thought. What is the right mix of awareness, interaction, and participation-building communications in your plan?

Now let's take a closer look at the specific goals, strategies, objectives, and tactics most commonly adopted by nonprofit communicators. Because the definitions of the various marketing strategies and objectives are new to many nonprofits, we'll spend the most time on those. We'll quickly summarize the goals and tactics, which are more widely understood.

If you get overwhelmed by all of the new vocabulary and definitions, don't worry. We'll go over a simplified plan next, in Chapter 3.

THE MOST COMMON NONPROFIT MARKETING GOALS

Marketing goals are the broad outcomes you seek via communications that help you achieve your larger organizational mission goals. In the nonprofit sector, a dozen goals represent the vast majority of the communications work. These 12 goals fall into four categories.

Community Engagement and Education Goals

- Engaging our community to keep people inspired by and active in our work
- Raising awareness of our issues to educate people on our cause
- Advocating on our issues to change hearts and minds

Brand and Leadership Goals

- Brand building and reputation management for the organization
- Positioning our staff as thought leaders or experts
- Communicating internally with our staff or board

Program Recruitment Goals

- Recruiting and engaging participants to use our programs or services
- Building our membership by recruiting and serving members of our organization
- Recruiting and engaging volunteers to help deliver our programs and services

Fundraising Goals

- Supporting fundraising from individuals making small to medium gifts
- Supporting major donor fundraising
- Supporting event fundraising (galas, walks, etc.)

It's common for communications staff to say they are expected to work on six or more of these goals simultaneously. Based on research from the

2019 Nonprofit Communications Trends Report, the most popular nonprofit communications goals are:

1. Engaging our community
2. Brand building and reputation management
3. Raising awareness of our issues
4. Recruiting and engaging program participants
5. Supporting event fundraising
6. Supporting fundraising from individuals making small to medium gifts

THE MOST COMMON NONPROFIT MARKETING STRATEGIES

The nonprofit sector employs a dozen different strategies, which are the marketing approaches used to achieve your goals. However, based on data first presented in the *2019 Nonprofit Communications Trends Report*, we know the sector relies heavily on four marketing strategies in particular: permission-based marketing, content marketing, event and experience marketing, and relationship marketing.

Permission-based marketing is sharing content with specific people who have signed up, subscribed, or otherwise agreed in advance to join your mailing lists and lists of social followers. Nearly all nonprofits use this strategy in some way by building opt-in mailing lists.

Content marketing is attracting people to your work and retaining their interest in it by creating and distributing content they find especially valuable and relevant. It is also sometimes called inbound marketing.

Just because you are doing permission-based marketing doesn't mean you are doing content marketing! You can send advertising content or appeals to your opt-in email lists. That's permission-based marketing, but not necessarily content they find especially relevant and meaningful themselves. Sending advertising and appeals are more in your self-interest, even though you have permission to do so.

You can also use content marketing independent of your permission-based marketing mailing lists. For example, when you add great content to your website, people can find it with web searches and read it without being opted-in to any mailing list.

Of course, you find the sweet spot when these two strategies work together. You send great content that keeps people on your lists, which allows you to also send them advertising or appeals without them unsubscribing or unfollowing.

For much more detail on content marketing, please read my book, the award-winning *Content Marketing for Nonprofits: A Communications Map for Engaging Your Community, Becoming a Favorite Cause, and Raising More Money* (Jossey-Bass, 2013).

Event or experience marketing is using frequent events or participatory experiences to promote your programs and services, encouraging in-person interaction between your organization, supporters, or program participants.

Sometimes this strategy is confused with the "supporting event fundraising goal." They are not the same thing.

If you are delivering programs and services via events and trying to get people to attend those events, then you are likely using permission-based marketing, content marketing, and general advertising strategies to market your events. Those events are programs or services and therefore your goals are more likely to raise awareness of your issues or to recruit and engage program participants.

If you are using events or experiences to market something other than donating, such as tours or happy hours to introduce new people to your organization, that's what I would consider an event and experience marketing strategy. The expectation is that the event or experience is merely the introductory first step in getting the attendees to do something else.

Relationship marketing is the fourth strategy most often employed by nonprofits. Relationship marketing is creating strong, long-term, loyal relationships with specific individuals and focusing on the quality of those relationships, rather than on individual transactions with those individuals. While the individuals will take a variety of actions in support of your nonprofit over the course of the relationship, their overall engagement with your cause is paramount. Major donor fundraising programs are often built on relationship marketing strategies.

In addition to these four most popular marketing strategies, nonprofits also use four additional marketing strategies that empower others to speak on behalf of the nonprofit, but in quite different ways: word-of-mouth marketing, peer-to-peer marketing, influencer or ambassador marketing, and partner or alliance marketing.

Word-of-mouth marketing is encouraging verbal or written recommendations or testimonials to be shared from one person to another. It relies heavily on casual, unplanned social interactions between people. Much of this will happen naturally on its own. But if you actively encouraging people to talk about you with their friends and family by giving them interesting things to share or asking people to post about you on review sites, then you are engaging in a word-of-mouth marketing strategy.

Peer-to-peer marketing is organizing and training volunteers to educate or advocate on your behalf. You work with individuals, but also support the community of peer educators or activists as a whole. Peer-to-peer fundraising gets a lot of coverage in our sector, but fundraising isn't always the goal. Get Out the Vote operations by political campaigns are another good example of peer-to-peer marketing.

Influencer or ambassador marketing is creating relationships with people with special influence or access to a broader group of people you wish to reach. Influencers can include celebrities, bloggers, market leaders, and anyone else who acts as a gatekeeper who decides whether to pass on your information to their communities. This strategy is especially important for nonprofits who are several steps removed from the people they are trying to affect in some way. A good example is an education think tank that wants to change how children learn in the classroom. They need to influence the professionals working in school districts to pass on their ideas to teachers in classrooms.

Partner or alliance marketing is cooperating with other organizations to jointly promote your cause generally or your specific products or services. It can include referral marketing, affiliate marketing, co-branding, and cause marketing. Examples of partner marketing include several nonprofits collaborating on a one-stop-shop service center for clients, private sector businesses referring customers to nonprofits or collecting donations at the cash register, and museums in a geographic area buying advertising together.

While these four strategies are similar, peer-to-peer marketing is much more organized and actively managed than word-of-mouth marketing. Peer-to-peer marketing also involves many more people than ambassador or influencer marketing. Partner or alliance marketing is typically accomplished through organizational relationships rather than through marketing to individuals.

To complete this list of a dozen strategies, you will also find some nonprofits using general advertising, search marketing, unsolicited direct response marketing, and location-based marketing.

General advertising is the placement of content into online, print, and broadcast channels meant to reach a targeted or general audience, rather than specific individuals. It can include everything from free flyers posted on bulletin boards to paid advertising in print and remarketing ads on social media. Remarketing is a way to connect again on a new site with people who previously viewed your content elsewhere. For example, if you shop online for a new couch on a website that has a Facebook tracking code embedded in it, then you may see ads for that same couch the next time you visit Facebook.

Search marketing is gaining traffic and visibility from search engines through both search engine optimization of content and paid search listings. Rather than just throwing content up on your blog or website, are you paying attention to what topics bring traffic to your site and writing to encourage the right kind of traffic? Are you managing Google advertising? If yes, you are doing search marketing.

Unsolicited direct response marketing is using mail, email, phone calls, and other communications tactics to communicate directly with people who have not previously opted in to communications with you. It is often used in direct mail acquisition fundraising with purchased or rented lists of names.

Location-based marketing is using mobile phone location data to provide messaging to people when they are physically near specific locations or when they use apps to check in at specific locations. It may also be called geomarketing and proximity marketing. We most often see this strategy used by nonprofits that run large public facilities like parks, zoos, and museums, where visitors can find detailed information about what they are seeing in front of them based on where they are standing.

THE MOST COMMON NONPROFIT MARKETING OBJECTIVES

Objectives are actions or steps you take to implement a strategy. These actions or steps are also what you measure to know if you are meeting your goals. Of all the goals, strategies, objectives, and tactics discussed in this chapter, we find the most diversity in the nonprofit sector when discussing marketing objectives.

That's because of the abundant opportunities to customize objectives to be SMART: Specific, Measurable, Achievable, Resourced, and Time-Bound. If you focus on creating objectives that are measurable and time-bound, you are usually also being specific. Ensuring that your objectives are achievable and resourced helps you stay within your capacity to actually accomplish the work.

In many cases, you should also add some reference to the *who* (your participants, supporters, or influencers) and sometimes to the *what* you are communicating about (your messaging or call to action) in order to customize the objectives in a meaningful way.

After coaching hundreds of nonprofit communications directors and teams, I've found that discussing, agreeing upon, and prioritizing specific objectives is the missing piece in the nonprofit marketing strategy puzzle. I strongly encourage all nonprofit communicators to spend more time working through the objectives in their plan than on goals, strategies, or tactics.

Our research at Nonprofit Marketing Guide first identified the 12 objectives most often used in the nonprofit sector in the *2020 Nonprofit Communications Trends Report*. Let's start by looking at the five most popular ones. Financial gains and participation levels are most common, followed by expressions of loyalty; change in knowledge or understanding; and people joining, subscribing, or following.

Financial gains or savings. To create a specific objective in this category, you might work to increase the percentage of 5K walk or run revenue raised via peer-to-peer fundraising by 20 percent. Or you might work to decrease your cost of acquisition for new donors.

Participation levels. A participation levels objective can be set when you are trying to increase registrations, donations, RSVPs, etc. For example, you might wish to sell out 90 percent of your workshops this year. Or you might wish to decrease the amount of time between when someone gets on your mailing list and when they take a specific participatory action like advocating for a policy change with their elected officials.

Expressions of loyalty. Loyalty is often judged in the nonprofit sector in terms of retention or renewals. Specific objectives could include maintaining a 75 percent donor retention rate this year. Or perhaps you would like to keep 50 percent of your email list highly engaged, according to a lead scoring tool in your constituent relationship management database.

Change in knowledge or understanding. This objective is best customized by being specific about changing knowledge or understanding within a specific group of people. For example, perhaps you desire to move 75 percent of beginners in your program to the intermediate level in six months. Website metrics, such as the amount of time returning visitors are spending on certain pages, could also indicate a change in knowledge or understanding.

Joining, subscribing, or following. This objective helps you measure list growth. It can be customized in many ways, such as increasing newsletter subscriptions by 20 percent this year, or optimizing email sign-up forms on your website to convert more visitors to subscribers, for example.

Nonprofit communicators may also consider additional objectives that attempt to measure the impact of their communications on how people think and feel.

Increased levels of influence. This objective would assess the extent to which your communications are increasing your influence with specific groups of people or increasing your share on the public conversation. For example, you might seek to get invited to speak at five industry events. Or you might try to improve your search engine rankings on 10 keywords. Or you may try to get your policy positions covered in five prominent media outlets.

Increased satisfaction. Perhaps you want your program participants, supporters, or influencers to feel more satisfied about their work with or relationship with your nonprofit. In this case, you might customize your objective to raise the Net Promoter Score for a specific program to +60. Or, if you use a lead scoring system to measure engagement of your email list, you might want to keep at least 35 percent of your list at a five-star engagement level.

Expressions of trust. You might wish to track whether your communications are leading certain groups of people to say or do things that demonstrate their trust in your organization. For example, you might want three new organizations to agree to partner with you on a new project. Or you may want 100 new participants to trust your nonprofit to help them address an especially difficult challenge.

Change in tone or attitude. You may be interested in tracking the extent to which communications help change the tone, sentiment, attitude, or preferences expressed by a group of people. In this case, you could work to move the majority of social media comments you receive from negative to positive. Or you could use feedback surveys or polls to gauge changes in attitudes or preferences over time.

Finally, nonprofits may also choose objectives that help measure the impact on how people behave.

Increased demand or desire. Are communications increasing requests, demands, or desire for something the nonprofit offers? For example, a health clinic may create a marketing plan to increase appointment requests by 30 percent next quarter.

Increased readiness or empowerment. This objective would help measure whether communications were helping certain groups of people be more ready or empowered to take a specific action. For example, you might develop a plan so that 70 percent of petition signers continue to open educational emails six months later. Or you might track the percentage of people who move from being aware of an issue to acting on it.

Change in behavior. If you want your communications to lead to measurable changes in how people behave, you might set an objective such as 50 percent fewer students engaging in behavior resulting in suspensions next semester.

It's worth noting that attributing some results, including behavior change and change in tone, specifically to a nonprofit's communications plan can be extremely challenging or expensive. It's unlikely that you'll be able to connect your communications directly and exclusively to those results.

Instead of drawing a direct link between your communications work and achieving an objective, we often speak instead in the language of Key Progress Indicators or Key Performance Indicator (KPIs). These are indicators of progress toward your goals and mission.

The tactics you use – the channels or type of content – can also influence how you phrase your objectives. I do caution you against only using objectives that are directly tied to a specific tool or communications channel. Ideally, you are using multiple tools or channels to achieve an objective.

THE MOST COMMON NONPROFIT MARKETING TACTICS

Tactics are easier to understand: it's all about the content you make and the channels in which you distribute that content.

Content includes all forms of writing and visual content, such as photography, graphics, and video.

Nonprofits especially interested in content marketing will likely create content in the form of downloads, problem-solving tools, and quizzes. Some nonprofits rely on content created by others through content curation or synthesizing data and information from others.

The most popular communications channels for nonprofits are:

- Websites and blogs
- Email, as single topic notices and appeals and as multitopic newsletters
- Social media
- Media relations or public relations
- Events, including hosted gatherings, presentations and public speaking, personal visits, and displays and booths
- Direct mail, including invitations, appeals, and print newsletters

Nonprofits also use:

- Paid advertising
- Signage
- Brochure, flyers, and other "leave behind" materials
- Additional online tools such as mobile apps and instant messaging
- Guest writing or syndication on other people's blogs or publications

OVERWHELMED BY YOUR CHOICES? SORT OUT YOUR PLAN WITH THE NONPROFIT COMMUNICATIONS STRATEGIC PLANNING CARD DECK

To make working with the goals, strategies, objectives, and tactics described in this chapter easier, Nonprofit Marketing Guide created the Nonprofit Communications Strategic Planning Card Deck. The double deck of playing cards, which includes definitions and examples, allows nonprofit communicators to visually lay out their communications plans. The card deck can also be used for a variety of planning and training exercises.

"When I begin to feel overwhelmed," says executive director Jeanette Stokes of the Resource Center for Women and Ministry in the South, "I can see all those cards spread out and realize that we can't do it all. I say to myself, 'Pick a goal and strategy and a few tactics.'"

Communications strategist Tara Collins feels the same way. "When planning a campaign, I restrict myself to just the three best cards for goals, strategies, objectives, and tactics so I don't get overwhelmed or sidetracked. The card decks allow me to lay it all out, shuffle, discard, reshuffle, focus and then get it all down on paper quickly."

The card deck is available at both Amazon.com and NonprofitMarketing Guide.com.

CONCLUSION: IF YOU CAN NAME IT, YOU CAN OWN IT

I use this quote from Pulitzer Prize–winning journalist and author Thomas L. Friedman in many of my trainings:

> "In the world of ideas, to name something is to own it. If you can name an issue, you can own the issue."[1]

Ineffective communications teams struggle with conflicting opinions and ambiguous interpretations of basic terminology. Effective teams, on the other hand, have a shared vocabulary that is clear and meaningful.

In nonprofit organizations where marketing is a fairly new or poorly understood concept, it's vital for communications staff to name and therefore own many important facets of the work. That includes naming the goals, strategies, objectives, and tactics described in this chapter. Doing so will help you build your team, be more strategic, and increase your effectiveness.

Nonprofit Marketing Plans in Theory – and in the Real World

"We used to use what I call the 'Oh My God' method of planning our communications," said Jeanette Stokes, executive director of the Resource Center for Women and Ministry in the South. "We'd look at one another and say, "Oh my God, if we don't tell people about this right now, it will be too late!" The chaotic creation of communications would ensure.

However, after Jeanette and her team began following the planning advice in this chapter, they felt much more organized and in control of their communications work. Even after their communications director left for another job, remaining staff were able to manage the communications work together. "We would have been completely disorganized in our communications to the public except for the editorial calendar. We make it, follow it, and know what each of us is supposed to be doing," said Jeanette. "We've been doing well enough in the absence of a staff person focused on communications only because of the editorial calendar!"

At Nonprofit Marketing Guide, we get asked all the time how to create a marketing or communications plan or strategy. But there isn't a simple answer, because it all depends on what you mean by those words: *marketing, communications, plan,* and *strategy.*

Several different documents, including an editorial calendar like Jeanette's, make up what we collectively call a marketing strategy and communications plan. Here's how we approach it.

WHAT GOES IN A MARKETING STRATEGY

I think of the marketing strategy as the document that answers the fundamental marketing questions that won't change much at all for the next one to three years. What are the marketing goals and objectives? Who do you need to communicate with most and what are the core messages to share with these people? What resources will be allocated to implement the strategy? A marketing strategy includes the following sections:

- Marketing goals
- Situational analysis
- Targeted communities
- Organizational brand or personality
- Messaging and primary calls to action
- Marketing strategies
- Marketing objectives
- Marketing tactics
- Resources

These sections are further defined in Table 3.1 and we will now look at each section more closely.

A BASIC, DEFAULT MARKETING STRATEGY

If you aren't sure where to begin, we suggest that you start with the most popular marketing goals, strategies, objectives, and tactics we reviewed in the previous chapter and build from there.

Goals: Engaging our community, brand building and reputation management, raising awareness of our issues, and supporting event fundraising.

Strategies: Permission-based marketing, content marketing, event or experience marketing, and relationship marketing.

Objectives: Joining, subscribing, or following; participation levels; change in knowledge or understanding; and financial gains or savings.

Tactics: Website and/or blog, email, social media, storytelling, earned media or public relations, events, and direct mail.

Table 3.1.
Elements of a Comprehensive Marketing Strategy

Plan Section	What the Section Includes
Marketing Goals	The primary marketing outcomes that support your organization's larger mission-oriented goals.
Situational Analysis	The conditions under which you must operate. Sometimes includes a marketing audit.
Targeted Communities	Who you must reach and convince; their interests, values, habits, and preferences.
Organizational Brand or Personality	How you wish others to perceive your organization through your communications.
Messaging and Primary Calls to Action	The specific messages that will move your audience to action.
Marketing Strategies	The best approaches to reach your marketing goals.
Marketing Objectives	The SMART steps you take to achieve a strategy. SMART is Specific, Measurable, Achievable, Resourced, and Time-Bound. Includes how you will measure progress.
Marketing Tactics	The tools, channels, and types of content you will use to pursue the objectives.
Resources	Resources required to implement the plan, including budget and staffing.

Marketing Goals

In this section, you define what you need to do or to accomplish.

What are your short-term and long-term goals? What do you want to achieve through marketing?

I suggest you begin with the twelve most common goals described in the previous chapter and winnow those down to what's most appropriate for your nonprofit.

The four most common marketing goals are engaging our community, brand building and reputation management, raising awareness of our issues, and supporting event fundraising.

Situational Analysis

Here you describe the conditions under which you must operate. This is also called an environmental scan. You'll also sometimes see a SWOT analysis – a review of the strengths, weaknesses, opportunities, and threats. Some strategies also include a marketing audit of existing communications work.

You may want to answer some of the following questions. What are the internal conditions under which your marketing program must operate? What are the external conditions under which you must operate? What partnerships can you rely on? What skills do you need, and which do you have on staff now? What systems need to be in place in order for your plan to succeed? What barriers must be overcome for your plan to be successful?

Who is the competition – who else is providing similar resources and information? Who is providing information or urging actions that are in conflict with your approach? Are there any myths that must be overcome? Are there any policies that will positively affect the outcome of your marketing plan? Are there any policies that could negatively affect the success of the marketing strategy?

Targeted Communities

In this section, you describe in detail who you are communicating with and what their interests and needs are.

What groups of people are you trying to reach? Within those groups, what are the specific subgroups of people who are most important to you? Who are some personas within the groups? What do these people care about? What's important to them? What's not important to them? What is their current level of interest in you and your issues? How much knowledge do they already have? What else do you believe they need to know?

Organizational Brand or Personality

Your organizational brand or personality is your identity and how others see you and feel about you. Brands are communicated through everything from word choices and visuals to the timing and location of your communications. Speaking in a unified organizational voice across all of your communications channels is an important part of your brand.

You'll want to create a brand and style guide that articulates all of the specific details (we'll discuss brand and style guides more in Chapter 15); however, your strategy should answer some basic brand questions. What is your organization really all about? What's your story? What makes you special? What will others associate you with? What tone, voice, and style best represent your nonprofit?

Messaging and Primary Calls to Action

In this section you lay out the specific messages that are most likely to work with your target audiences. You'll answer questions like these.

What are you trying to get people to do? What kind of installment plan or baby steps can people take along the way? What's in it for them? Why should they care, and why now?

Given your target audiences' interests, needs, and values, what specific messages about you and your work are most likely to resonate with them? What messages or approaches would they be most likely to ignore? What kind of information do the specific groups want to receive from you?

Marketing Strategies

In the previous chapter, we reviewed the twelve most common nonprofit marketing strategies. These are the marketing approaches you will take to achieve your goals.

The four most common marketing strategies are permission-based marketing, content marketing, event or experience marketing, and relationship marketing.

You can customize these strategies by being specific about which targeted communities each strategy will be used to reach and which programs or services you will market with each strategy.

Marketing Objectives

In this section, you define your marketing objectives, which are the measurable steps you take to implement a strategy. We encourage you to make your objectives SMART: Specific, Measurable, Achievable, Resourced, and Time-Bound. As you add the details to make your objectives SMART, you will be referencing the earlier sections of your strategy on your targeted communities and your messaging and primary calls to action.

What specific measures are available to track the effectiveness of the marketing campaign? Which measures are of primary importance and which are secondary? How often will you review and report on the metrics? How will the metrics influence adjustments to the plan? What's impossible to measure, but still important to consider, perhaps through anecdotal information? Are there any unstated or hidden expectations that need to be addressed?

The most popular objectives for nonprofits fall into these four categories: joining, subscribing, or following; participation levels; change in knowledge or understanding; and financial gains or savings.

Marketing Tactics

Here you describe the tactics you will use to deliver your messages to your audiences. Think about questions like these.

What communications tools should you use to deliver messages to the target audiences? How specific and personalized should communications be? Who should deliver the message? Will you use offline tactics, online tactics, or a combination? How often should your audiences receive the messages via any given communications channel? Where should these messages appear?

The most common communications tactics are websites and/or blogs, email marketing, social media, storytelling, earned media or public relations, events, and direct mail.

Resources

In this section, you outline the financial and staffing resources required to implement the plan. You may wish to answer the following questions.

What financial resources are required? Where will these resources come from? Do they exist today, or do they need to be developed? What staffing resources are required? Do you have the skills and time needed on staff? Or do you need to hire new staff and consultants/freelancers? Do you need to recruit volunteers to perform certain tasks? Do you need to enlist the support of various partners to implement parts of the action plan?

What elements of the plan will be scaled back first if adequate resources are not available? What elements of the plan should be expanded or accelerated first should additional resources become available?

WHAT GOES IN A COMMUNICATIONS PLAN

While your marketing strategy focuses on big strategic questions and answers that will not change frequently, your communications plan is a much more dynamic and living set of documents that are constantly adjusted and updated.

When we talk about communications plans, we are most often referring to some combination of three different documents: The Big Picture Communications Timeline, an editorial calendar, and creative briefs.

Big Picture Communications Timeline

A Big Picture Communications Timeline maps out all of the events and milestones (both within and beyond your control) that will drive your communications in the coming year, along with your primary calls to action and the major storylines you want to share. It's completed with all parts of the organization in mind: programs, fundraising, and marketing/communications. My second book, *Content Marketing for Nonprofits*, contains a full chapter on Big Picture Communications Timelines and you can also find additional information at NonprofitMarketingGuide.com.

Editorial Calendar

An editorial calendar is your day-to-day working plan and what I consider to be the most important of all of the documents discussed in this chapter. At a minimum, an editorial calendar outlines what you are sharing, in what communications channels, and when. You can add much more detail, including who is responsible for what, internal deadlines and workflows, and more.

Editorial calendars can take the form of spreadsheets or calendars. Whether you have "spreadsheet brain" or "calendar brain" – which format allows you to work more productively – is up to you.

An editorial calendar, along with your Big Picture Communications Timeline, will help you keep track of what's called the story arc. Although each communications piece should be able to stand on its own, it's also helpful if you view each article or video as part of a larger story that you are trying to tell. Using an editorial calendar can help you map out that story arc, or how the story will progress or evolve over time.

Ultimately, you'll work toward creating a master editorial calendar that includes everything that's being created and published in a given time period. However, in practice, many nonprofits find it easier to begin editorial planning with just a subset of their communications.

You can ease into editorial planning by setting up your editorial calendar in several different ways.

By channel. Create a separate editorial calendar for each major communications channel that requires a significant amount of content, such as your newsletter or blog. You can also create an editorial calendar for your social networking presence as a whole.

An editorial calendar for a quarterly print newsletter could have the standing heads or placeholders for the different types of articles you typically include in your newsletter (for example, success story, donor profile), as column heads. The publication date of each issue would run as row heads in the left-hand column (see Table 3.2 for an example). You would then fill in the grid with the specific article details for each edition, such as the name of the program that the success story would come from and the name of the donor who would be profiled.

Or let's say you want to create a weekly social media calendar to ensure that you are updating your status and contributing to the conversations on a handful of sites throughout the week. You would put each of the sites (Facebook page, Twitter profile, and so on) across the top row and the days of the week down the left-hand column. Now you can fill in as many boxes as you like with the topic you want to talk about or the kind of update you want to share (say, retweet three times, post a discussion question on the Facebook page).

By audience. You can also organize editorial calendars by audience. If you have multiple, distinct audiences (such as teachers, parents, and students) and you want to ensure that you communicate with them regularly, you might create a calendar for each audience with your channels down the side and your time frames across the top. If you have several groups of people who you're trying to reach out to and you're concerned that your communications may

Table 3.2.
Sample Editorial Calendar for a Print Newsletter for a Local Humane Society

Article Category	Spring Edition	Summer Edition
Program Success	Spay/Neuter campaign results	How we increased our cat adoption rate
Donor or Volunteer Profile	Bill Miller – How he brokered the deal for the free dog food	Shondra Smith – How she got teenagers to volunteer at the shelter
Adoption Profile	To be decided – recent dog adoption	To be decided – recent cat adoption
Pet Tips	Preparing pets for a new baby	Hot weather tips for outdoor pets
How You Can Help	Volunteer with the dog-walking program	Invite us to speak to your community group
In Every Issue: Pets Available for Adoption, In-Kind Donations Wish List, List of Donors Since Last Issue		

unconsciously favor one group or other, this method will help you find the right balance.

By program. You can also organize editorial calendars by program if you have several different programs and you want to make sure that you are spending an appropriate amount of time communicating about each one. Just as with the audience-oriented calendar, you can list your program across the top and dates down the side, then fill in the boxes with channels and specifics about the content you'll deliver there.

Creative Brief

The third type of document that could be considered a communication plan is a creative brief. A creative brief is a quick worksheet that you fill out before you get started on any significant piece of communications work. It's like a mini strategy for a particular campaign or project.

Using a creative brief forces you to consider important questions before you get started. It's also a wonderful collaboration tool that helps your team work out potential conflicts before you spend a lot of time on the project. It's also a nice touchstone that you can return to if you feel like a project is going astray at any point.

Here are common questions in a creative brief worksheet:

- What is it? What is the deliverable?
- What is the goal or purpose of the communications piece?
- What is the single most important thing it should communicate?
- Who is the communications piece for (specific participant or supporter groups, for example)?
- What is the specific call to action?
- Is there a specific voice, tone, or style for this piece that should be reflected in copy or design?
- What gap is this piece filling in our existing communications line-up?
- How will success of the piece be measured?
- Who is the primary decision maker on this piece? Who else is working on it?
- What budget and additional resources will be made available?
- What are the deadlines for the first, intermediate, and final drafts?

You can find much more detail and examples of Big Picture Communications Timelines, editorial calendars, and creative briefs in my book, *Content Marketing for Nonprofits: A Communications Map for Engaging Your Community, Becoming a Favorite Cause, and Raising More Money*, as well as at NonprofitMarketingGuide.com

Example: How to Use These Three Planning Documents Together

By using these three planning documents together, Melissa Cipollone, the communications strategist for Pasa Sustainable Agriculture, has greatly improved the efficiency of the organization's publication production process.

"I start the planning at the beginning of each year, where I work with all of our staff to create a Big Picture Communications Timeline for the year," said Melissa. "Then I schedule creative briefings with staff as needed, where we work together to fill out a creative brief." This guides their brainstorming process and focuses the conversation on important decisions such as the purpose of each publication, its intended audience, its backward production timeline, etc. "We also clearly define roles, such as who are reviewers, who are approvers, who will design the layout, etc.," said Melissa.

Next, she adds the production timelines to a shared Google editorial calendar, so everyone involved in a production can see the agreed-upon deadlines. "Having a shared editorial calendar also lets me easily show others where we might encounter bottlenecks or conflicts with other planned projects," said Melissa.

Finally, she initiates a production and editing process that includes clear steps. These are: (1) creating an outline; (2) reconciling a "global" draft, where they only focus on the content and structure of a piece; (3) reconciling a "local" draft, where they hone in on sentence-level edits; and (4) copyediting and proofreading to polish everything up.

"Creating a streamlined planning and production process has helped me work more collaboratively with our staff, and reduce conflicts," said Melissa. Before, staff would realize that their visions were misaligned after a lot of time was already spent on a draft, or they wouldn't account for the time needed to allow peer reviewers to participate in the production process. "It's certainly not a fool-proof process, but it's helped us tremendously," said Melissa.

NONPROFIT MARKETING THE QUICK-AND-DIRTY WAY

Although drafting a comprehensive marketing strategy and communications plan that answers the scores of questions posed here is ideal, the reality is that this kind of thoughtful, well-researched, and well-considered plan is out of the reach of many organizations, perhaps including yours. You may not have the time or staff cooperation to pull it off. If so, you'll turn instead to the quick-and-dirty approach that focuses on the three most important questions in nonprofit marketing:

Who are we trying to reach? Define your targeted communities or groups. Get as specific as you can about your target audience. Everyone or the general public aren't good answers.

What's our message to those people? Explain what you want them to do and why they should do it, or why they should care.

How do we deliver that message to those people? Pick the right channels to deliver your message to your target audience.

Nonprofits without communications staff always have the answer to the third question. We need a flyer! We need a billboard! We need to be on Snapchat! Your challenge is to always introduce the first two questions into the conversation: Who is this for and what do we want to say to them or ask them to do?

Once you get those basics into the conversation on a regular basis, you can add two other questions:

So what? This gets to the "why?" question for your target audience. Why should this message or call to action matter to them? What's in it for them to follow through? Think of these questions from their point of view, not yours. This is how you build out the messaging that goes with your call to action.

Why now? Even if you have convinced your target audience that your messaging and call to action make sense, they still need a nudge to do it now. How can you create some urgency so people will stop doing everything else and follow through on your call to action?

EXAMPLE: THE AMERICAN RED CROSS'S "DO MORE THAN CROSS YOUR FINGERS" CAMPAIGN

The American Red Cross wants every household to do three things: to get an emergency kit, to make a communication and evacuation plan, and to be informed about the disasters that are common in their communities. That's their product. Fair enough, but how are they going to make it happen?

Although the American Red Cross has the resources to develop comprehensive marketing strategies complete with healthy amounts of audience research and environmental analyses, I asked Mark Ferguson, who managed the "Do More Than Cross Your Fingers" campaign several years ago for the American Red Cross, to share the marketing strategy for the campaign in the quick-and-dirty format.[1]

Defining the Audience: Moms with Kids at Home

The Red Cross's historical research and experience shows that moms with kids under 18 living at home are especially receptive to messages about disaster preparedness. No surprise there – if anyone is going to care about the nest and the babies in it, it's Mom. But some research also showed that 82 percent of moms say they drive household purchases. So, if you are trying to get a family to organize a disaster preparedness kit that will most likely require some purchases, reaching out to the people who decide what to buy makes sense.

Creating the Message: Testing the Campaign Slogan

But what do you say to a busy mom to get her to make this a priority? It was important for the Red Cross to come up with a message that spoke to moms but that also had broader appeal to the American public at large. Even if moms were the target, the message needed to be appropriate for a much wider audience as well. It was also important, said Mark, for the message to start from where people were and to help them move forward with their family disaster planning, regardless of how much they may have already done. Through their research, they knew that about 80 percent of families had taken one of the three key steps (getting a kit, making a plan, or staying informed), and this campaign was about moving them to take another.

To come up with the right message, the Red Cross hired the firm Catchword Branding, which specialized in naming. They provided a thousand possible slogans to the Red Cross, many of which were simple variations on one idea. Using a cross-functional team (marketing, development, disaster preparedness, field staff, and so on), the Red Cross whittled the list down to the best five. Those five were then tested through an online survey with Harris Interactive to find which one resonated best both with moms and with the public at large.

Of the five options, said Mark, one was in the form of a question and one played on the "heroes" theme that the Red Cross has used successfully before. Another one was deemed too snarky or too clever (survey respondents said it just didn't sound like the Red Cross). The chosen theme, Do More Than Cross Your Fingers, stood out among the five with both moms and the public at large. "It was fresh," said Mark, "but not in any way offensive."

Delivering the Message: Going Where Moms Are and Using Voices They Trust

With a message in hand, the next decision was how to get it out to moms. "We knew that moms are really active online," said Mark. Thus, the campaign centered on www.redcross.org/domore, and all of the other online and offline tactics pointed back to that page.

The Red Cross also wanted to emphasize that each family is different, so what's in their emergency kits should be different too. Thus, one of the key components of the website was a game called Prepare 4 that helped you build your own personalized kit.

"One of the goals was to make disaster preparedness simple and interesting," said Mark, "not just a brochure or a ho-hum shopping list. We wanted something interactive and friendly." During the game, you'd answer questions that helped you build a kit that was customized for your family, right down to including something fun for the kids to do while the power is out. At the end of the game, your list of items was emailed to you so that you could go gather up the items from around your house and go shopping for what was missing.

You could also share what you included in your personal kit with others in a My Kit section, as spokesperson Jamie Lee Curtis did on the site via video. The selection of Curtis as the spokesperson was another move that connected well with moms.

The Red Cross also reached out to "mommy bloggers" who had blogged about disaster preparedness before. They pursued coverage in traditional print magazines focused on women and parenting. Marketing partnerships with Clorox and FedEx (brands many moms use regularly) rounded out the campaign channels.

CONCLUSION: ALWAYS THINK BEFORE YOU SPEAK

No matter how big or how small your nonprofit may be, asking yourself the three basic questions behind a Quick-and-Dirty Marketing Plan will help ensure that you are headed in the right direction:

- Who are we trying to reach?
- What's our message to them?
- What's the best way to deliver that message?

Creating a marketing plan *before* launching into tactics, however simple the plan (even if it's nothing more than answers to these questions on the back of a napkin), is always a smart approach. It's as true for nonprofit marketing as it is for disaster preparedness – you have to do more than cross your fingers!

How Nonprofits Increase Their Marketing Effectiveness Over Time

Over the last 20 years working in nonprofit communications, Courtney Kassel, chief communications officer at the Liberty Hill Foundation, the largest social justice foundation in Los Angeles, has seen big changes in how nonprofits approach the work.

"Nonprofits have come to understand how important marketing and communications are to their overall success, and they are placing a greater emphasis on the core skills and training needed to be successful," said Courtney. "Outdated notions of just getting anyone on the team to send out a press release and calling that work 'communications' are finally evaporating in the face of data that shows that marketing and communications is a critical field that requires similar levels of commitment to continuous learning and improvement as any other field."

Courtney's organization places a great deal of emphasis on professional development and she works to ensure her team members have access to training on the latest best practices and evolving technology in our field. Networking also provides her team with opportunities to stay connected to colleagues across the industry and to share their learnings with others.

Some of the data Courtney is referring to comes from Nonprofit Marketing Guide's annual *Nonprofit Communications Trends Reports*. Several editions of the report confirm that about one-third of nonprofits consider their communications work "very or extremely effective." What's the difference between that third of nonprofits and the other two-thirds who are less effective? And what needs to happen for a nonprofit to move into the "very or extremely effective" third?

41

At Nonprofit Marketing Guide, we set out to answer those questions and based on our research, developed what we call the "Five Levels of Nonprofit Communications Effectiveness." These levels are a function of both the skills and experience of the individual staff and the marketing maturity of the nonprofit as an organization. They reveal the typical path that nonprofits follow as their marketing and communications functions mature over time.

LEVEL ONE – BEGINNER

At this level, you'll find people new to nonprofit marketing and communications who need an introduction to the profession and basic nonprofit marketing concepts.

You may be a Beginner if . . .

- You are trying to understand basic nonprofit marketing concepts and what it means to be a nonprofit communications staffer.
- You are likely focused on talking about the organization, rather than what's most relevant to the community.
- You probably feel like a huge to-do list was dropped in your lap without much guidance.

LEVEL TWO – CAPABLE

At this level, you'll find people who are trying to get a handle on what's included in the job of a nonprofit communications coordinator or director. Your focus is very tactical: How do I get the work done? At level two, you are starting to think about planning, building more consistency in your communications schedule, and creating messaging that is more relevant to specific target audiences. But these goals often seem out of reach because you are overwhelmed more days than not by just trying to get things done.

You may be Capable if . . .

- You are seeing the need for more planning and consistency.
- You are struggling to get everyone in the office on the same page.
- You spend time looking for quick fixes.
- You are starting to help others connect the dots between their work and yours but may still feel like communications is quite isolated.

LEVEL THREE – SKILLED

At level three, your confidence is growing, and you are starting to think more strategically about the work. For example, you are working more collaboratively with others in your organization and trying to manage an editorial calendar. You are incorporating best practices like storytelling and content marketing into your work. While you still might feel like you are more reactive than strategic, you are working toward managing the communications functions at your nonprofit, rather than feeling like the job is running you. You are pressing your organization to limit communications priorities – and are more willing to push back when something clearly isn't a priority.

You may be Skilled if . . .

- You are ready to start proactively managing the communications work by implementing editorial planning.

- You are building a collaborative culture and communications strategy is regularly blended into other conversations.

- You likely still have a long list of target audiences, but you are getting more savvy about creating and repurposing content.

LEVEL FOUR – ADVANCED

At level four, you are stepping up to lead the communications work at your organization. You are firmly in control of editorial planning and developing workflows and systems that keep you grounded and focused. You are interested not only in doing the work well but in measuring performance and improving results.

You may be Advanced if . . .

- You've built trust in your work and the role of communications in your organization is better understood and appreciated.

- With that support, you are able to invest resources where needed and to implement more sophisticated approaches.

- You are managing the organizational brand and working with others on style and tone consistency.

- Decision-making roles, accountability for deadlines, and team structure and development are clear and in place.

- Your content is getting the desired reaction and your effectiveness is easier to document.

LEVEL FIVE – EXPERT

At this level, your communications work is very strategic and focused. You've mastered the basics and are now implementing and refining your strategies, trying to optimize your work. You have the capacity to create high-quality, targeted content distributed across highly coordinated channels. You make good communications decisions quickly and others trust your judgment. You can experiment freely and pursue tactics that communications departments with less support or experience can only dream of. You are managing the brand at all levels.

You may be an Expert if . . .

- You are improving your nonprofit's overall effectiveness by refining and optimizing your marketing strategies and tactics.

- Your content strategy is highly coordinated and fully integrated across multiple channels.

- You measure results and experiment with confidence.

When we look specifically at four elements of nonprofit marketing work, we can see how that work becomes more sophisticated as nonprofits advance through these five levels.

Let's take a closer look at these four elements:

- How much planning is taking place and what kinds of documents are created

- How well permission-based marketing is managed, including list building and list segmentation

- How well content creation and content marketing are managed

- How well the organizational culture supports marketing and communications

HOW MUCH PLANNING IS TAKING PLACE

The Quick-and-Dirty Marketing Plan focused on answering the three questions (Who are we talking to? What's our message? How do we deliver that message?) is all the nonprofits at the Beginner level can manage. As they move to the Capable level, they will try a Big Picture Communications Timeline. At the Skilled level, they are working on managing an editorial calendar.

At the Advanced level, we see more creative briefs and campaign-level planning. We often don't see a fully integrated marketing and communications strategy until the Expert level.

HOW WELL PERMISSION-BASED MARKETING IS MANAGED

Permission-based marketing is the number one strategy for nonprofits. Non-profits at the Beginner level are usually still working on understanding the basic concepts of opt-in list building and segmenting. They are often still fighting the notion that there is no such thing as "the general public" in marketing and want to reach everybody with every message.

As they reach the Capable level, they will start discussing the concept of target audiences and what it might look like to create communications for them instead of the general public.

At the Skilled level, they begin working on prioritizing those target audiences and better understanding them through the concept of personas. These nonprofits will also be thinking about different types of list building and engagement campaigns that could work for their organizations.

At the Advanced level, the nonprofit is fully using personas or other tools to understand their targeted communities and are actively segmenting their lists to share the most relevant content with each segment. We also see more advocacy for investment in better tools to create content and manage communication channels so that they can experiment with more sophisticated list building and engagement campaigns.

Finally, at the Expert level, nonprofits implement highly targeted campaigns and build engagement and segmenting automation into their constituent relationship management (CRM) software. They also consistently implement sophisticated list building and engagement strategies.

HOW WELL CONTENT MARKETING IS MANAGED

Content marketing is the second most important strategy for nonprofits.

At the Beginner level, nonprofits first focus on their calls to action: What do we want people to do after they are aware of us and our issues? They are also building an understanding that communications channels like email, social media, and print aren't separate, but part of one system.

At the Capable level, nonprofits will spend time learning about what their community finds most compelling and relevant and start to incorporate more of that into their content.

They will also explore some of the basic best practices for their primary communications channels, such as how email writing is different than print, and how the various social media channels differ. We often see an interest in learning the basics of nonprofit storytelling and supporter-centered copywriting at this level.

At the Skilled level, nonprofits will take a harder look at the content they are creating and start making big changes so their communications are more relevant and targeted. They will examine their primary communications and think more strategically about what content really works best where. As they do so, they will likely want to improve their skills in writing microcontent (headlines, subject lines, and the like) and more engaging lifestyle writing (e.g. social media content).

Once nonprofits reach the Advanced level, they will hone their content marketing strategy by better defining their core topics (what they most want to be known for) and exploring their thought leadership potential. At this level, staff are always thinking about content in terms of how it will work across multiple channels.

At the Expert level, more sophisticated techniques like advertising retargeting come into the content marketing strategy. These nonprofits are also working on content and channel optimization. For example, they likely know which content produces what results and what needs work based on experiments and data, rather than guessing.

HOW WELL ORGANIZATIONAL CULTURE SUPPORTS MARKETING

At the Beginner level, nonprofit communications staff are often still helping leadership understand that nonprofit communications is a specialty that requires full-time attention.

As they reach the Capable level, they will talk more with others about the core concepts of targeted communities, messaging, and appropriate communications channels. We also see the introduction of some best practices and tools of the trade. Many communicators are focused on building trust in their tactical competence at this level.

As they move into the Skilled level, communicators begin to ask for more strategy and they also practice saying "no" more often and pushing back on requests that are not priorities. Good organizational habits begin to take hold, such as using an editorial calendar and creative briefs in meetings. Skilled staff also start creating style guides, templates, and other tools that staff can use as they begin to think of themselves as a communications coach for other staff. They also begin focusing more on their own personal productivity, which sets them up to work on team productivity next.

At the Advanced level, editorial conversations are taking place at all levels of the organization and are coordinated by the communications staff. Brand guidelines and work on organization style and tone consistency is underway. Communicators at this level are also building trust in their ability to make good judgment calls and they seek more say in larger organizational strategy. At this level, communications staff are also focusing on better ways to measure their progress.

Finally, at the Expert level, staff are quite agile, making good decisions quickly and being very responsive all while remaining strategic. They have no shortage of great content because they are repurposing and omnichannel masters. They experiment freely and measure results well.

CONCLUSION: GIVE IT TIME AND PUT IN THE WORK

You can't create an effective nonprofit communications program overnight. Both the staff and the organization as a whole have to grow into it. However, we do know the likely path for that growth, from Beginner to Expert. Take it one step at a time, and build knowledge into proficiency, and proficiency into expertise.

Do Your Homework: Listen to the World Around You

For many years, the American Friends Service Committee (AFSC), an advocacy organization that mobilizes people to create social change, assumed that it had two distinct audiences: activists and donors. The staff spoke to these audiences using different voices and engaged them with different types of content.

However, as Beth Hallowell, AFSC's director of research and analytics, and her team began listening in earnest to their community of supporters through interviews; surveys; focus groups; and website, email, and social media analytics, they made what felt like a startling discovery: What they had assumed were two separate groups, activists and donors, were actually the same people.

"Through these studies, we learned that our donors saw their contributions to AFSC as part of a lifetime of activism," said Beth. "We learned that we had misidentified many of our supporters as single-issue activists, when in fact, they were interested in a variety of social justice issues." Activists were either donors too or highly likely to become donors in the future. "By listening to and understanding our supporters, we have transformed our approach to segmentation and content creation," said Beth.

You don't need to be a director of research and analytics to go through many of the steps that Beth and her team took to learn more about the people you are, or hoping to, communicating with.

Whether you call it listening, intelligence gathering, or market research, you need to pay attention to what's happening in the world around you. Your nonprofit doesn't operate in a bubble, so pretending that it does will only hurt your organization and make it impossible to successfully market your cause. Your communications will be received within the context of everything else that is happening in the worlds of those receiving them.

This advice – to do your homework and to listen before you create and implement a communications plan – may sound like simple etiquette, but it's really about much more than that. A good listening network should serve as a cornerstone of not just your marketing program, but also how you manage your entire nonprofit organization. What you learn through listening should shape the way you approach your mission and how you design and implement all of your various programs – not just your marketing or fundraising. Listening helps at every level: it can help your professional community thrive, your organization prosper, your individual programs grow, and your own personal career soar.

Every day presents an opportunity to learn more about the people you are trying to help and the people who are trying to help you. If you listen closely, you will learn a great deal from the simple personal interactions that take place in and around the office every day. But in addition to this ambient listening, you should also put in place a more formal listening structure or network that allows you to keep the two-way flow of information between you and others open and moving.

Your listening network should include both in-person and online tools. It should include data generated by others (such as national polling data) and data you create specifically for your organization (such as evaluation forms that participants complete after an event). It should include participating in social media channels where people are connecting, conversing, and collaborating with others, regardless of time zones or geographic boundaries.

WATCH AND LISTEN

When getting to know a group of people, whether they are program participants or major donors to your cause, nothing works better than talking directly to members of that group. Although formal focus groups with two-way mirrors and trained facilitators or national telephone surveys may be some of the most effective ways to learn about your targeted community, they are also expensive. Don't consider formal research unless you have a minimum of $10,000 to spend. The good news is that informal research, which is either free or affordable, works just as well for most organizations.

To learn more about a particular group of people, simply go talk to some people who fit the description of that group. Hang out where they are. In every conversation that you strike up, ask a few questions that help you learn more about what's important to them, what their days are like, what infuriates them, and what makes them laugh. Get to know them as people, before you start to think of them as potential clients or supporters.

Do the same kind of watching and listening with your current clients and supporters. Take them out to lunch and learn everything you can about these people. Ask them directly: What is it about your nonprofit or your cause that motivates them to be involved? What is it about your nonprofit that your donors, volunteers, and other supporters find so compelling? The answers may surprise you.

For example, I used to serve on the board of a local HIV/AIDS support and case management organization. At a meeting shortly after I joined the board, each of us explained why we wanted to serve on this board. Being new and knowing only a few other board members before this meeting, I suspected that the majority would give reasons related to disease prevention or to a personal experience with HIV or AIDS.

Although that was certainly a motivation for several people in the room, most of us (including me) focused instead on wanting to fight for the underdog, the people society would rather turn away from. It wasn't HIV, per se, that motivated us as much as the impact of the stigma of HIV on people in the Southern rural counties where the nonprofit operates, and our desire to fight that discrimination. If we polled our donors and other supporters, I suspect we'd hear similar comments.

Hearing perspectives like these from your targeted community can be incredibly helpful when it comes time to sit down and write a newsletter or a fundraising appeal letter, or to recruit new members to the board. It gives you a big head start in creating messages that will appeal directly to their values.

CONVENE INFORMAL FOCUS GROUPS

You don't need a two-way mirrored conference room to hold a focus group. Instead, invite six to twelve people to come by your office. Better yet, find a location closer to where they are. Offer them a meal during the day or dessert and coffee at night. It's easier to draw conclusions from informal focus groups if everyone in the room is a member of a particular target group that you have previously defined (for example, limited to parents of high school students you hope will enroll in your after-school driver safety program, rather than including people without children or with only very young children).

Develop a discussion guide of four to six questions per hour, up to two hours per session. Broad questions about experiences, like "Tell me what happens when . . ." and "What would you do if . . ." can get the conversation going, without pointing it in too specific a direction. Make sure your focus group facilitator understands the issues and questions but can remain completely neutral during the discussions. It's important that the participants don't think you are looking for particular answers. They may want to please you and tell you what you want to hear, which is actually not helpful at all!

In most cases you'll want to record the session so you can review it again later. It's also helpful to ask participants to make their own notes about the questions you are asking before the conversation really begins, so you have a record of those first impressions as well.

Sarah Durham, founder of Big Duck, a nonprofit communications consulting firm in New York City, often works with clients to conduct informal focus groups. One client, a community development organization that served the residents of several public housing developments and ran numerous social service programs, had a problem: the people who were using their services the most didn't live in the particular public housing developments they were targeting. Although people were using their employment assistance programs, they weren't the people they were trying to reach.

To find out why the right people – the public housing residents – weren't using the programs, Big Duck helped the organization conduct five informal focus groups. The focus groups were to be held in the on-site community centers in each development, and a few days before the focus groups, program staff actively recruited residents to attend. Participants received a free dinner and discussed the kind of services they needed and what they knew about the nonprofit organization.

As they talked with the residents, the organizers had what Sarah calls a big "Aha!" moment. The nonprofit had been using traditional advertising methods to spread the word about their free programs, including advertising on garbage cans, posting flyers, and hiring people to hand out postcards describing the services they offer. What they heard in the informal focus groups was that the residents were suspicious of anything marketed as "free" by people who appeared to be strangers. They figured there had to be a catch, so they ignored the advertising.

In response to what they learned through these focus groups, the nonprofit completely shifted its marketing away from the blitz of generic outreach and toward more personal one-on-one testimonials from current program participants. They found that the most effective way to bring a new participant into the program was to have a current participant share her or his success story with that person and to accompany them to the program office.

The nonprofit also shifted toward holding block parties where people who have graduated from the program speak about their experiences and bring their friends. Not only is the new approach more effective in recruiting the right people, but it also costs less than the old way of hiring people to stand around thrusting postcards toward passersby.

CONDUCT ONLINE SURVEYS

If you have a good email list or a large enough web or social media presence, you can use free or affordable online survey tools to collect data. Online surveys allow you to easily calculate quantitative (numerical) data by seeing how many people answer multiple choice questions in a particular way or rank various choices. You can also collect qualitative data (anecdotes) through open-ended text boxes. Although these are harder to compile, it allows your survey respondents to answer in their own words, which gives you valuable insight into the vocabulary they use and the way they describe certain situations.

One challenge with online surveys is ensuring that your questions are not leading or loaded. In other words, you don't want the way your question is worded to push respondents toward one answer over another. Online survey providers often supply tips to their customers on how to write good questions and how to use their tools most effectively.

You may wish to collect demographic data as well, such as gender, age, or location. This allows you to analyze your data in different ways so you can compare how different subsets of your targeted community responded to your questions.

Perhaps your biggest challenge will be limiting the number of questions you ask. Think through what you will do with the answers you get to each question. What will you learn and how will that change the way you do your work? Eliminate questions that are simply "nice to know."

ANALYZE YOUR WEBSITE, EMAIL, AND SOCIAL MEDIA STATISTICS

You can also learn a great deal about your community by reviewing how they use your online content. Whether looking at your website, email, or social media channels, all online platforms provide at least some level of analytics about its users.

For example, by reviewing Google Analytics or whatever analytics package is installed on your website, you can get a sense for which search terms people are using to find your website. Website analytics can also tell you which pages visitors are staying on the longest and the pages through which they entered and exited your site. All of this gives you a better sense for the types of content people are interested in.

Your email service provider gives you information about who is opening your emails and clicking on the links within them. This can signal which topics people are interested in, much like your website analytics. But you can also go further by measuring your email engagement rates. Engagement metrics give you a sense for what portion of your mailing list is opening a lot of your email – and are thus much more interested and engaged in your work – and what portion is only casually or mildly interested.

Social media metrics, often displayed under an "Insights" tab, will typically provide some basic demographic data on your followers as a whole (e.g. breakdowns by age, gender, and location). The advertising tools within each platform typically provide even more details, such as relationship status, education level, how frequently they use the platform, and on what kind of device.

You can also track which topics and posts get the best engagement on social media. Sometimes you can deduce who your followers are based on the type of content that gets the most engagement. You may find, for example, that people seem to prefer basic or introductory content compared to more sophisticated and advanced content (or vice versa). From that, you could deduce that your social followers are new to your cause if they like the basic content more. Or they might be more experienced if they like the more expert content.

You may see that certain topics or types of posts get much more interest. Do posts about using your services get more engagement or do posts about the results of your work get more engagement? The first might indicate that participants in your programs are following you, while the second might indicate donors are following you. Combined with other information you have from operating your programs and services or meeting your donors at events, you may be able to use that information to make some guesses about the type of people who are following you on social media.

REVIEW MEDIA KITS AND ADVERTISING

Media kits can also be very helpful. If you know that your targeted community reads a particular publication or uses a certain website, obtain the media kit for that publication or site, which you can often find online in the "About," "Advertising," or "Partners" section of a media outlet's website. Media kits show potential advertisers the demographic information about the readers of that publication or users of the website. They are trying to convince advertisers to pay them money in return for reaching a certain demographic. You can use this same data to better understand those people in your targeted community who read that publication. Media kits are often available online, although you sometimes need to request one directly from the advertising sales department.

WATCH FOR RELEVANT POLLING AND SURVEY DATA

Many national polling and survey companies share data online via blog posts, press releases, and free reports. Excellent sources for the nonprofit sector on consumer behavior include the Pew Research Center's Internet & American Life Project, the Harris Poll, and MRI-Simmons.

FIND CONVERSATIONS VIA KEYWORDS AND HASHTAGS

By performing keyword or hashtag searches, you can find and track what's being said on websites, blogs, social media sites like Twitter and Instagram, online bulletin boards or discussion sites like Reddit, and more.

Keyword research is most often associated with search engine optimization (which we'll touch on in Chapter 11), but it's also useful for listening. You want to know who, where, and how other people are discussing the topics you care about.

Start by creating a list of keywords and hashtags related to the work you do. If you are at a loss for where to begin, look in your website analytics for the keywords that people are using in searches that lead to your website. Go to the Instagram and Twitter profiles of similar organizations to yours and see which hashtags they use most frequently.

Once you've been listening for a while through your keyword or hashtag searches, you can develop a list of people who often talk about issues you care about and start following them directly. Subscribe to their blogs and follow them on their social media channels. The same goes for specific places on the web, such as news sites or blogs with multiple authors.

WHAT TO DO WITH WHAT YOU LEARN

You can use what you learn through your listening to create personas, empathy maps, and journeys, which is the subject of the next chapter.

However, the benefits of listening don't end there. Here are many more concrete steps you can take to use what you learn from listening.

Build Your Network and Connect More Directly with Your Community

Better understand the people who matter most. Find, follow, and listen to the people who you think match your targeted community, whether they are potential clients, funders, donors, advocates, or volunteers. Learn more about what interests them, what kinds of questions they have, and the language they use, so you can communicate with them in more meaningful ways. It's basic market research, and if you listen for no other reason, you will still find it worthwhile.

Start conversations with potential new supporters. See who's talking about your issues. Look at what else those people are saying online. If you think these are individuals who would be interested in what your organization does, reach out to them with a personal message. Offer information or resources or invite them to an event. Open the door to a relationship, just as you would to a personal friendship.

Find new partners. Discover who else is interested in and working on the same things you are, especially people and organizations you otherwise might never have known existed (for example, they do what you do, but on the other side of the country). Share your successes, replicate theirs, and create new partnerships to get more done.

Create Better Content

Be more relevant. If you want to be considered a player in the space you are working in, you have to be relevant. And to be relevant, you have to understand where people are *right now*. Listening helps you keep up with what's happening to the people who matter to your organization's success.

Answer questions and provide suggestions. People are constantly posing questions and talking about the challenges they face online. Answer questions, offer suggestions, and become known as a good source of information and assistance.

Spot programmatic trends earlier. By consistently listening to the "raw feed," you'll be able to pick up on trends related to your work long before they solidify into conventional wisdom. You can adjust your programs accordingly, and when others finally catch up, you'll be considered on the cutting edge.

Knock down your writer's block. Not sure what to write about in your newsletter or blog? Read what others in your community are talking about and then write about the trends you see, draft a response to something you found particularly interesting or offensive, or summarize the best points others are making on a particular topic.

Measure the success of your communications. Are you trying to get the word out? See how well the message is spreading by monitoring who's passing it on to others and how the message is changing as it spreads.

Keep tabs on your critics. Even if you choose not to respond directly now, keeping up with what your critics are saying will help you develop better rebuttals and fine-tune your messaging in the future.

Encourage More Engagement on Your Issues

Feed your biggest fans. Build personal relationships with your biggest supporters online and give them what they need to spread the word about you (for example, great stories, photos, videos, inside scoops on what's happening in your field). These are the people who will not only introduce you to their friends and expand your circle of supporters but also stand up and defend you and your cause if attacked by others, so keep them on your side.

Find your niche. It's a competitive world, even for nonprofits (some might say *especially* for nonprofits when financial times are tough). By listening to what's going on in your professional world, you'll have a much better understanding of where you fit in, where you can fill gaps, and how you can stand out. And you *must* stand out – that's what nonprofit marketing is ultimately all about.

Respond rapidly to flare-ups. Listening puts you higher up in your own personal fire tower, so when a potential firestorm sparks, you can douse the flames much faster than if you were on the ground, miles away.

Correct misconceptions. Is someone confused, misinformed, or worse, spreading rumors? Try to set the record straight by presenting your point of view in a nonconfrontational way.

Give good customer service. If your nonprofit is in the business of providing direct services, the people you serve are not unlike customers at a commercial establishment. Many corporations and the consumers they serve use social media as a near-constant, real-time way to answer customer questions and address complaints.

Expand Your Personal Knowledge and Capacity

Learn the lingo. Learn what words your targeted community is using. The language that your clients use, for example, is often very different from the language that professionals in the field use. The reverse is true too: if you are trying to break into a professional community, listening is a good way to pick up on some of their jargon and buzzwords.

Increase your own professional knowledge. Identify the leaders and big thinkers (I call them the "big brains") in your field; keep an eye on the issues they are discussing and the resources they are recommending. It's like attending a professional networking event without leaving your desk.

Pick up a reality check. We all make assumptions every day, but when you assume too much, you know what happens? "You make an *ass* out of *u* and *me*." (I thought that was so profound when I first read it at age ten!) Road test your assumptions by putting them out there and listening to the responses you get.

CONCLUSION: NEVER STOP LISTENING

By listening to the world around you, you'll have a much better understanding of what's happening in your field, and you'll know where you should engage in conversations with supporters and other people important to your success. Listen to learn who's talking about your issues and your organization, where the buzz is building, and what your supporters are excited about, whether you ever see these people in person or not. People are talking about the issues you care about and even about your organization and staff. The question is whether you'll listen in and how you'll respond to what you hear.

PART TWO # Answering the Three Most Important Nonprofit Marketing Questions

In Part Two, let's go deeper into the three Quick-and-Dirty Marketing Plan questions. In Chapter 6, we'll explore how to define the community you want to reach. In Chapters 7, 8, and 9, we'll explore your messaging, focusing on what kinds of messages work best for nonprofits, including storytelling and gratitude. We'll wrap up this section with Chapter 10, where we'll look at how and where to share your messages with your communities.

chapter SIX

Define Your Community: Who Do You Want to Reach?

Second Sense is a nonprofit providing client-centered support and training to people with vision loss in the Chicago area. It used to be called Guild for the Blind. "After 50 years, our name was dated. We felt it deterred some people from seeking services with us," said Cheryl Megurdichian, the development and communications director.

As part of the renaming process, Cheryl's team conducted focus groups with current and past users of their services. While discussing the old name, a focus group participant steered the conversation to how the nonprofit's staff referred to people in the room. "We had called the people we serve 'consumers' for years," said Cheryl. "This participant stated how much she disliked that term. And, to our surprise, the rest of the participants shared her view."

What to call the group of people the nonprofit served wasn't originally part of the conversation. However, using welcoming language was the whole point of the renaming exercise. "The fact that the term we used to talk about the people we help was viewed negatively by those people was a huge concern," said Cheryl. As a result of this discussion, Cheryl's team did a separate survey of their program participants asking them to vote on the term they preferred. Second Sense now refers to the people it serves as "clients," the overwhelming choice of the people they serve.

As Cheryl discovered, how you refer to people affects your relationship with them. That's why I find the term "target audience" distasteful, even though it's the most well-understood and frequently used term for the topic of this chapter: narrowing down and understanding the different groups of people your nonprofit is communicating with. "Target audience" is a holdover from a time when most marketing communications were one-way advertisements. However, the concept behind the phrase is still extremely relevant: you need to focus (target) your messaging to specific groups of people. But it's a mistake for nonprofits to think of them as an audience.

I encourage you, like Cheryl did, to come up with terminology for the people you are communicating with that's a better fit. One term I use is PSI, which is an abbreviation for participants, supporters, and influencers. I also use the words "community" and "segments" in place of "audience." And yes, sometimes I still use the phrase "target audience" especially when I feel it's the quickest way to get my point across.

IN MARKETING, THERE'S NO SUCH THING AS THE GENERAL PUBLIC

The first question in any strategic marketing conversation – and in the Quick-and-Dirty Marketing Plan described in Chapter 3 – is defining who it is you are trying to reach. The alternative – skipping this step and creating outreach and fundraising campaigns for the general public – is a complete waste of time.

The reality is that most people will never, ever care about your mission enough to help your organization. The general public includes high school seniors and octogenarians. It includes single parents living on public assistance and business moguls living in high-rise penthouses. It includes liberals, conservatives, and people who have never voted in their lives and probably never will. They should all care, every single one of them, about child abuse, global warming, and your good cause too. But they don't. No magic number of flyers or YouTube videos or Facebook friends will change that.

Maybe that sounds like bad news. But here's the good news: If you focus your limited marketing resources on the people who really do matter most to your organization's success, you'll spend a lot less money and time, and you'll get better results. You'll actually make a difference.

Defining and narrowing your community (or your participants, supporters, and influencers) has other benefits too, like minimizing office squabbling and hand-wringing. Once you define who you are communicating with and learn all you can about them, the answers to questions like "What should we put in the newsletter?" and "What color palette should we use on our website?" all become much easier to answer, because you'll know exactly who you are writing and designing them for.

RECOGNIZE THAT YOU ARE COMMUNICATING WITH MULTIPLE GROUPS OF PEOPLE

So just who are these people who matter most to your success? Your challenge is to categorize them into specific groups, or segments, held together by common characteristics or values.

At a minimum, most nonprofits have two segments: the people they serve in some way and the people who support that mission financially. But a portion of your clientele or volunteers may also be donors. Sometimes these groups do overlap, as we saw in the previous chapter with the American Friends Service Committee's donors and activists. In those cases, it makes more sense to use other factors beyond their relationship to your cause to define the segments. We'll look at some of those factors next.

But other times, the groups are vastly different. You may run a homeless shelter, but the people who donate to you may have never set foot in one. Because of these different segments, your marketing can sometimes go in what feels like divergent directions. One of my favorite examples of how nonprofits who understand and target specific groups can be wildly successful with extremely specific targeting comes from the 2008 presidential election where Barack Obama was running against John McCain.

Ari Wallach was the co-executive director of the Jewish Council for Education and Research (JCER), a political action committee. He was surprised to see Barack Obama hovering at only 60 percent of the Jewish vote in summer 2008 polls. In past presidential elections, Jews had overwhelmingly chosen the more progressive candidate. JCER had created JewsVote.org to support its advocacy for Obama, but after seeing these lower-than-expected polling numbers, Wallach knew they needed to do something more.

By using connections and keeping it simple, JCER produced TheGreatSchlep. com, including a now infamous video featuring comedian Sarah Silverman, for less than $50,000.[1] In the video, Silverman recalls how "Gore got f***** by Florida" and how it would be "the Jews' fault" if Obama lost the election. And those were the tame parts. It's fair to say that the ultimate target for this campaign – older Jews living in Florida – would have found the video distasteful, if not completely appalling.

But the video wasn't created for them. It was created for their twenty-something grandchildren – young, progressive, Comedy Central–loving Jews with contacts in Florida – who Wallach saw as the ideal carriers of the pro-Obama message. It worked. The site went viral, was covered by the major networks, and raised more than $250,000 in less than four months. But more importantly, it mobilized thousands of young Jews to talk to their grandparents about Obama. According to the national exit polls, Jews voted for Obama over McCain 78 percent to 21 percent, and he won Florida convincingly.

This campaign was wildly successful because it targeted a very specific segment important to the cause (older, progressive Jews living in the battleground state of Florida who were hesitant to vote for Obama), with a message that was meaningful to them (Obama is the best chance for a president who supports the same policies that they do), delivered in a package they couldn't resist (a visit, or at least a call, from their grandchildren).

That's what you need to do too, but in your own way, and probably minus the profanity.

SEGMENT YOUR COMMUNITY INTO GROUPS

You can use several techniques to break down the "general public" into more manageable and more meaningful groups.

Basic Demographics

Are most of your target community men or women? How old are they? Do they live or work in certain places? Are most a particular ethnic group? Is income or education level relevant? Also consider factors that define how they spend their time. Where are they, and what are they doing there, from 9:00 a.m. to 5:00 p.m. or on weekends? What is their family status? Do they rent or own?

Behaviors and Psychographics

What is this group of people (perhaps independent of demographics) doing or not doing related to your cause? Think about your calls to action. Are they doing the right thing, but in the wrong place or at the wrong time? Social change comes about by individuals within a group changing their actions, so what kind of behavior changes would you like to see members of this group making? What do they think? Does this group of people tend to have strong likes or dislikes?

The Stages of Change

If you are trying to convince people to modify their behaviors in significant ways (say, to quit smoking or to recycle more), the stages of change may be a helpful way to break down your target community into smaller groups. The stages of change are known more formally as the transtheoretical model in health psychology.

The first stage is precontemplation, in which the individual doesn't yet acknowledge that a problem exists. Next is contemplation, in which the individual acknowledges the problem but has plenty of reasons why they can't be addressed. Preparation comes next, in which the individual says, "Okay, I'll give it a try." This is also known as the testing phase. Next is the action phase, in which the individual is ready and makes the change. The final stage is maintenance and relapse prevention, in which the individual works to make the behavior a habit. Table 6.1 presents some examples. The questions and needs of someone in the contemplation stage are quite different from those of someone in the maintenance stage, which means your marketing approaches to those two groups would be quite different too.

To illustrate this process, let's say we run a community center that operates a variety of different programs, including a family computer lab, after-school tutoring and recreation for teens, and meal delivery to homebound seniors. Our

Table 6.1.
The Stages of Change

Stage	Description	Typical State of Mind
Precontemplation	Does not recognize problem and has no intent to change	"Not my problem."
Contemplation	Recognizes problem, considering action	"I'll think about it."
Preparation	On the verge of taking action to make a change	"I need to do something. I'll give it a try."
Action	Making changes	"I'm ready. Let's do it."
Maintenance	Trying to maintain those changes	"I'm sticking with it."

professional staff manages the programs, but we rely heavily on volunteers to implement the programs day to day. We are funded through a diverse mix of government contracts, foundation grants, and donations from individuals and service organizations (for example, church group and civic club donations).

Rather than asking the "general public" to "support" our "programs" – three phrases so generic that they are essentially meaningless – we decide to break down our target community into several groups. We start first with a behavior we are seeking: volunteering. We further refine this, using the stages of change, to people who are in either the contemplation or preparation stages. They know these needs exist in our community and that our nonprofit is working to address them, but they don't think volunteering is right for them for some reason, or they have considered volunteering but haven't actually contacted us yet.

We take it one step further by breaking down our group into four subgroups, defined by what we have historically understood to be the primary motivation for volunteering with our organization: retired people who want to stay active, people who are trying to build their résumés, people who want to give back to their communities, and people who want to change the world.

USE PERSONAS, EMPATHY MAPS, AND JOURNEYS TO MORE CLEARLY DESCRIBE YOUR GROUPS

Breaking your target community down into groups can feel impersonal. You add personality back into the process by creating personas within your groups. Empathy maps and journeys can elaborate on those personas.

Personas are good examples of individuals who are typical of the larger group. They are vivid narrative descriptions of individual people, real or imaginary, who are members of the group. Be specific as you describe each persona. Give each an age (not an age range), a name, income and educational levels, hobbies, and so on. Find a stock photo to represent each individual persona. You may create three or four personas per group.

Where do these three or four people come from? Start with your gut reaction. If you've been working in the field or for your organization for a while, you'll probably have a good sense for who the members of this group are. You can supplement your gut reaction by asking others who also work with the group for theirs and by observing the group in action.

Next, to build out this character, explore what each of these personas values most. You are no longer thinking about the general public. You aren't even thinking about the larger group or your cause. Instead, you are thinking about the values of these three or four individuals. What's important to them in their daily lives?

Here is a small sample of the kinds of values you might assign to your personas:

Time	Status	Cooperation	Pragmatism
Sleep	Power	Idealism	Privacy
Convenience	Fitting in	Safety	Connecting
Adventure	Change	Money	Independence
Public recognition	Self-help	Efficiency	Teamwork
Good karma	Competition	Challenge	Predictability
Control	Action	Peace and quiet	Fun
Love	Formality	Compliance	Exclusivity
Openness	Learning	Spirituality	Exhilaration

An empathy map is a visual tool to help define or supplement your persona. Empathy maps come from "design thinking" and visually articulate how a particular type of person thinks and feels. It's often created during a group exercise so that staff can empathize with the person they are serving or communicating with.

The map typically identifies the person in the center, which sections around the center labeled to identify what that type of person says, thinks, feels, and does during the day. Some empathy maps label these quadrants in slightly different ways, such as think, feel, see, say, do, hear, pain, and gain. Google "empathy map images" to see a variety of completed examples (Figure 6.1 shows one example).

With agreement on your personas and/or empathy maps, you can construct the journey for each persona. User journeys or story maps are most often found in product or software development but are easy to adapt to nonprofits. They are a visual timeline that describes the relationship between a persona and your organization, highlighting the phases or stages where different interactions take place. For example, if the stages of change discussed earlier are relevant to you, then you might use a journey template like Table 6.2. You can name the phases

Figure 6.1.
Empathy Map

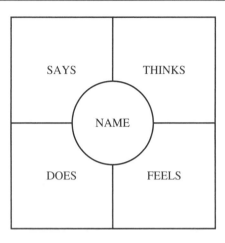

Table 6.2.
Sample Persona Journey

Persona Name

Stage 1	Stage 2	Stage 3	Stage 4	Stage 5	Stage 6
"Not my problem"	"I'll think about it"	"I need to do something"	"I'll give it a try."	"I'm ready. Let's do it."	"I'm sticking with it"

Add what your persona is doing, thinking, or feeling in each stage here.
Add what your staff are doing internally at each stage here.

or stages whatever you like, such as Awareness, Interaction, and Participation or Get on Mailing List, Attend Event, Donate. Google "customer journey map images" for many examples.

Journey maps are often split into external and internal journeys, so that you can see what's happening inside your organization with your staff as your personas are interacting with you from outside the organization. This can be as simple as a flowchart or drawn into something more akin to a path on a map.

AVOID CULTURAL STEREOTYPES

Creating groups and personas is by definition a form of stereotyping. There's no way around that. Your challenge is to ensure that you are describing characters who are truly representative of the group. Although they should be stereotypes of the people most important to the success of your organization, be sure that you are not inadvertently assigning characteristics that are false cultural stereotypes or tropes.

This is particularly dangerous when a nonprofit's staff have little direct experience with the specific type of persona they are creating. For example, several years ago, I worked on creating a set of personas with a community-based health organization. One of the personas we were working on was a drug-abusing, low-income woman.

Several of the staff members had degrees in social work and public health, but had no direct experience working with low-income, female drug abusers. Their initial characterization was what someone in the room crassly called a "crack whore" – a skinny, fidgety woman with dirty clothes and hair, always looking for someone to sell her body to for the next fix.

Then another staff member spoke up. He had abused drugs himself at one point earlier in his life and had worked with this kind of persona often over the last several years. The picture he drew was quite different. The persona he described was someone who tried to look presentable most of the time so that she could hide her addiction from the people around her and hold down a part-time job. Although she would still trade sex for drugs, it wasn't something she did daily. After much discussion, the group decided that this persona was much closer to the organization's clients than the misleading stereotype they had started with.

WATCH FOR GATEKEEPERS AND CREATE PERSONAS FOR THEM, TOO

In some cases, to reach your ultimate target community, you may need to go through someone else first. Think of this person as the bouncer at a hot nightclub, an agent representing a celebrity, or even a community foundation representing hundreds of donors. They control who and what flows through to the other side, where your real target community is. Analyzing the needs and interests of the gatekeepers can be just as important to your success as reaching your intended target community. You may need to create separate personas for the gatekeepers too.

For example, if you run a sports program for children, you need to get the kids excited about playing so you'll describe the activities in ways that emphasize fun, friends, and competition. But you also need to convince the parents to enroll their children in the program and pay the fee. Although the parents also want their kids to have fun, they are more likely to be concerned about you providing a safe learning environment, and your marketing materials should address those interests and concerns.

If you want to reach out to twentysomethings about preventing sexually transmitted infections, you may literally run into bouncers. One of the most effective ways to deliver your message is to go where your target community already is, especially when they are making decisions related to your issue. Therefore, if you wanted to reach people who may be considering having unprotected sex with each other, your job will be easier if you develop cooperative partnerships with club owners and bar managers. To convince those people to allow you to put beer coasters with safe sex messages on the bar and a condom display in the bathroom, you first have to address their concerns about hassling their customers and interfering with their sales.

EXAMPLE: CREATING SPECIFIC PERSONAS WITHIN A SEGMENTED GROUP

Let's create four personas, one for each of the subgroups that we believe represent our most likely new volunteers. We'll describe them as specific people, whether real or imaginary.

Anna represents our retired person who wants to remain active. She is a 70-year-old Chinese American boomer. She and her husband, Frank, ran several small businesses in the community over the years and were actively involved in the Chamber of Commerce and other civic groups. But since retiring a few years ago they have turned all of that over to their children and business partners. Anna is pursuing some new passions, including watercolors and pickleball. Frank has cancer, and Anna is his primary caregiver.

What does Anna value? She values predictability and time, because she is pursuing other passions, but also taking care of her sick husband. She used to be a mover-and-shaker in the business community and misses some of that visibility, so she also values some public recognition.

Jessica represents our résumé builders. She is a 32-year-old African American divorced mother of two girls, ages five and eight. She works full-time as an administrative assistant, but the pay is hourly without good benefits. She would like to build her project management skills so that she can apply for executive assistant jobs that are salaried, with benefits. Her ex-husband is still in the girls' lives, but he travels for work so he is not a reliable source of childcare. As is true for most single parents, time, money, and convenience are extremely valuable to Jessica. Self-help is essential to her long-term goals for her family, and spirituality is also a major part of her life.

John represents our volunteers who want to give back. He's a white male 64-year-old boomer who's living a comfortable upper-middle-class life with his wife, who is a homemaker and volunteer extraordinaire in her own right. His two kids are doing well in private colleges, and he looks forward to having grandchildren to bounce on his knees in a few years. He wears a suit and tie to work at the bank every day, but changes into a golf shirt and shorts as soon as he gets home. John feels lucky to have what he does, even though he believes he has earned it. He wants to give back, but on his own terms. He values efficiency and control.

Miguel represents our volunteers who want to change the world. He is an idealistic 19-year-old Latino who is fluent in both Spanish and English. His parents immigrated here when they were about Miguel's age and have told him many stories about the poverty they endured as children in their native countries. He is attending community college, because he isn't sure what he wants to do with his life yet, but he hopes to transfer to a four-year college the year after next. He has many interests, and they change often, so he's not likely to commit to anything long term. At the moment he's into hip-hop, baseball, and hanging out with his friends. Miguel values fun, fitting in, and making the world a better place.

Can you imagine some ways that the journey maps for each of these four personas would align and how they would be different? Would they learn about your organization in a different way? Would they have different expectations for a good volunteer experience? As a result of their differences, would they interact with different people on your staff? All of these questions and conversations will help you create more appropriate and relevant communications plans for volunteer recruitment.

EXAMPLE: MATCHING VOLUNTEERS WITH THE RIGHT OPPORTUNITIES

Bridget Bestor, a volunteer development specialist with ADVOCAP, which helps people and communities reduce poverty and increase self-sufficiency, encourages you to think about what your own volunteer selfie would look like. What would you be doing in the photo you took of yourself volunteering for your favorite cause?

Now, think about the people who you hope are going to volunteer. Do you know what their selfies would look like? Understanding that is part of understanding them and knowing how to provide the right volunteer opportunities for them.

"When someone is searching online for volunteer opportunities, they see position descriptions crafted to fit the needs of the nonprofits, not their needs as a volunteer," said Bridget. "The same process often happens in person when a potential volunteer visits with a volunteer coordinator. The coordinator is quick to tell the potential volunteer what time slots are available or sell them on an opportunity that sorely needs more volunteers to meet the organization's needs."

As Bridget points out, while this may seem reasonable from the nonprofit's point of view, it does little to help the volunteer find an opportunity that's meaningful to them. "Volunteers have a picture in their mind of what volunteering looks like to them. We need to find out what is in that picture," said Bridget. She suggests an initial get-to-know-you conversation before talking about specifics. "The first question I ask is, 'When you walked in here today to search for volunteer opportunities, what was the picture you had in your mind of what volunteering would look like with you in it?' I always get an answer and that answer is a great starting point to making sure you find the right match," said Bridget.

Of course, you still want to have a variety of choices for your volunteers to pick from. You may have opportunities that they didn't know existed. But listen first. "I can't tell you how many times I have seen a spark in someone after I explain a particular volunteer opportunity that resonates with them because I listened first," said Bridget.

CONCLUSION: DON'T JUMP AHEAD TO TACTICS

In the rush to get everything done, many nonprofits jump straight to tactics without first considering who the target communities for those tactics are. If you find yourself struggling with tactical questions, go back to square one: Who are we trying to communicate with and what do they care about?

You will inevitably have multiple communities with different values, needs, and interests. But if you work through the process of defining both your groups and your personas, you will be able to see the points where your communications to each of them can overlap into one multi-community strategy and where you will likely need to create separate, specialized strategies. Each community, for example, may receive the same message, but packaged in a different communications tactic (for example, you reach one group through mainstream media publicity; you reach the other primarily through word-of-mouth messages spread through faith communities). Or each community group may get its own message through its own communications channels, yet those separate messages work together well to create progress toward your mission (for example, doctors get one message at their offices about talking to their patients about cancer prevention; patients get a different message at home about talking to their doctors about cancer prevention).

But you can't make these important decisions without first working through what makes your community and the segments within it special and why a relationship with your cause would be meaningful in their lives.

Create a Powerful Message: What Do You Want to Say?

When the COVID-19 pandemic struck in 2020, the Atlanta Humane Society began hearing a lot of concern from their community about what people would do with their pets if they were one of the tens of thousands who seemed fine one day only to be hospitalized the next. "As an organization, we were concerned too," said Christina Hill, the director of marketing and communications.

The Atlanta Humane Society was used to messaging about pet preparedness each year in the late summer and fall during hurricane season. But they felt they needed a different, more engaging, and hopeful way to get people to think about who would care for their pet should they get sick during the pandemic – and quickly.

"We decided to play off a mix of godparents and a bridesmaid ask box," said Christina. (A bridesmaid ask box is typically a gift box with a message inside from the bride-to-be to the recipient asking, "Will you be my bridesmaid?"). Thus, the "Will you be my furry godparent?" campaign was born.

The digital campaign included fillable social media images that people could use to ask their friends or family to be the caregiver of their pet in an emergency. "We encouraged our community to fill it out, tagging their caregiver, and tagging us in their Instagram Stories for a chance to win a swag bag," said Christina. They also produced a video blog showing people how to put together their furry godparent ask box and fill it with fun little gifts and important things like their pet's medical records that would be needed by a furry godparent in case of emergency.

"It felt great to change our normal 'Be prepared!' ask to a more direct 'Act now!' message and to see the community engage and start the conversation around who would care for their pet in case of emergency," said Christina. Based on the campaign's success during the pandemic, the Atlanta Humane Society expects to reuse the theme during hurricane season and as a regular reminder to the community to always keep their pet's emergency plans in mind.

Why did this campaign work so well? And how do you get members of your target community to help you with the big problems you are trying to solve? You have to make it personal and meaningful to them, as Christina and her team did.

We've looked at how to get away from the general public so that you can market to specific groups of people and personas who are most important to your nonprofit's success.

Now it's time to craft messages that connect personally. The most powerful messages used by nonprofits embody at least one of these characteristics (and the Atlanta Humane Society used several of these):

- They emphasize the impact on one person, animal, or thing.

- They evoke specific emotions.

- They reinforce personal identity.

- They validate a decision or action by appealing to reason.

- They have a clear, strong call to action.

THE POWER OF ONE OVER MANY

On May 10, 2007, *New York Times* oped columnist Nicholas Kristof wrote a now-classic column called "Save the Darfur Puppy."[1] He lamented that publicizing the suffering of a puppy with big eyes and floppy ears would do what the suffering of hundreds of thousands could not: motivate the world's leaders to end the genocide in Sudan. Many experienced fundraisers thought to themselves, "You know, he's right."

The psychological research that Kristof quoted in his column backs up what veteran fundraising copywriters know too: Asking someone to help one person (or one puppy) is likely to produce more action than asking that person to help thousands of people.

Research by Paul Slovic of Decision Research and the University of Oregon showed that people who are otherwise caring and would go out of their way to help another individual become numb and indifferent to the suffering of the masses.[2] In one experiment, people were given $5 to donate to alleviate hunger overseas. The first choice was to give the money to a particular child, Rokia, a seven-year-old in Mali. The second choice was to help 21 million hungry Africans. The third choice was to help Rokia, but as just one of many victims of hunger. Can you guess which choice was most popular?

Slovic reported that donations to the individual, Rokia, were far greater than donations to the second choice, the statistical portrayal of the hunger crisis. That's not particularly surprising. But what is surprising, and some would say discouraging, is that adding the statistical realities of the larger hunger problem to Rokia's story significantly reduced the contributions to Rokia. Giving the donor the larger perspective didn't work.

A follow-up study allowed donors to give to Rokia or to a hungry boy named Moussa. Both Rokia and Moussa attracted similar levels of donations. But when given the option of donating to both Rokia and Moussa together, contributions fell off 15 percent. In another experiment, donors who were shown a photo of eight starving children contributed 50 percent less money than those who were shown a photo of a single child.

We are more compelled to act when we feel a direct connection with one person or one living creature we can help. You may recall the starfish story. On a beach where thousands of starfish have been stranded, an old man is throwing them back into the ocean. A young man walking by tells the old man, "You can't possibly make a difference." As another starfish lands safely back in the sea, the old man replies, "It makes a difference to that one." And he keeps picking them up and saving them, one by one.

The motivating power of focusing on just one works in many ways in nonprofit marketing. You need to speak to each of your supporters as individuals. You need to speak about the impact of their donations on other individuals. And you need to speak as an individual working on this cause, rather than as the monolithic nonprofit organization. Good nonprofit marketing is about creating and building the relationships between these individuals, as well as the network or community of support you create when you add all of these relationships together.

THE POWER OF EMOTIONAL CONTENT

If you ask veterans of hard-fought political campaigns which matters most – what a person *feels* or what a person *thinks* about your candidate – they will tell you, without exception, that heart overrules head in the voting booth.[3] The same goes for the way we make purchasing decisions, the way people vote on juries, and whether we support charitable causes.

As described in *Brand Immortality: How Brands Can Live Long and Prosper* by Hamish Pringle and Peter Field, the UK-based Institute of Practitioners in Advertising analyzed 1,400 case studies of successful advertising. They compared the profitability boost of ads that appealed primarily to emotions versus those that relied on rational information like statistics. Ad campaigns with purely emotional content outperformed the rational-only content by two to one. Ads that were purely emotional also performed better than ads with mixed emotional and rational content, though by a much smaller margin.

These results affirm the findings of Dr. Robert Heath of the University of Bath's School of Management. He found that US and UK television advertisements with high levels of emotional content made the advertising successful, not the message itself. The emotional ads enhanced how people felt about brands being advertised. Ads with low levels of emotion had no effect, even when they were factual and informative.

We want to *feel* good about what we are doing, so we make decision with our hearts (or guts) and then analyze selective facts in our heads to justify those decisions. But which emotions motivate us the most? Best-selling author and marketer Seth Godin said the three most important emotions in marketing are fear, hope, and love.

Many studies, especially in the social marketing community, have shown that fear can motivate people to change their behaviors, but only when it's clear that the threat to themselves or loved ones is real. Ways to avert the threat must also be clear and doable. Otherwise people are likely to be both defensive and dismissive of your message.

Although fear-based messaging is usually used in a negative way – "This bad thing will happen if you don't take this action" – you can also accept fear as one of the characteristics of your target community and then offer them positive ways to overcome that fear.

That's one approach that the staff of Alberta Health Services in Medicine Hat, Alberta, took when trying to increase the number of women getting screened for cervical cancer. The staff met with groups of women in informal focus groups and listened to their fears, which included that the screening would produce a positive result for cancer and that unskilled health providers with clumsy hands would be performing the Pap tests.

Based on what they heard, the staff redrafted the clinic's marketing messages, so that they helped free women from those fears. One key message was ". . . because I want to know that everything is okay." Images emphasize the comfort of dealing with skilled and qualified health professionals.

The clinic quickly introduced the negative they already knew was there, but then dismissed it with a positive point of view, getting beyond the issue immediately. Within five months, the staff turned a stale and sterile direct mail campaign into one that motivated so many women that appointment slots were booked six weeks in advance.

What about the power of love and hope? Most fundraising experts will tell you that's what they prefer too if you are in it for the long run. Although messages that induce fear may work in the short run and with new donor acquisition, donors will quickly tire of your "the sky is falling" tactics. Shift to more hopeful messaging, especially for donor retention communications.

THE POWER OF PERSONAL IDENTITY

How supporters feel about themselves in relation to your cause, as well as the stereotypes associated with your cause and your messaging, will also affect how likely they are to support you. Several studies have shown, for example, that when Asian girls are asked to identify their gender on a math test, they don't do as well (because of the stereotype that girls aren't good at math). But when they are asked to identify their ethnicity, they do much better (because of the stereotype that Asians are good at math). The role of personal identity in how we make decisions and behave is another important factor for you to consider as you develop messages for your target communities.

Can you tap into the personal identity of a segment of your supporters and use a link to your organization to affirm that identity? Describe what it is like to be in their shoes, then see if you can find a natural connection to your organization. "I am a [describe the person's identity] and therefore supporting this cause feels entirely natural to me because [explain how it reinforces the person's identity]."

Take, for example, the idea of being a fighter for what's good and right. Nonprofit work is often a fight against something or someone bad in the world, and in just one month in 2019, I saw fighter messaging coming through loud and clear. The American Kidney Fund used the tagline, "Fighting on all fronts."

Planned Parenthood Action Fund asked supporters to "fight for laws and policies to protect your rights and health." United Way asked supporters to learn more about the "fight to end hunger and food insecurity." The Humane Society of the United States asked people to "join the fight" to protect animals in puppy mills and research facilities. The ACLU asked website visitors to pledge to be monthly donors to "fuel the fight" against the Trump administration. The list goes on and on. These organizations were hoping that people would say to themselves, "Yes, I am a fighter and therefore supporting this cause feels entirely natural to me, because I want to fight to eliminate [kidney disease, puppy mills, etc.] too."

I'll share another personal story about the power of identity. I have given to my alma mater, the University of California at Berkeley, one time and one time only. Since I graduated way back in 1991, I've received countless letters highlighting the academic achievements of some very smart, usually male and much older than me, scientists and engineers on the campus. Problem is, I don't understand half of what they are talking about. Although I'm a fairly analytical person, I despised physics, and my only C at Cal was in astronomy.

But in the fall of 2007, I received a colorful direct mail piece from Cal that blew me away.[4] On the cover, it asked, "Who are you? Cal alumni are . . ." The "you" was in big, bright yellow letters, standing out against a black background. As I opened the piece and unfolded it, I saw a series of panels:

- Movement Leaders & Story Weavers
- Creators & Innovators
- Educators & Crusaders
- Trendsetters & Friend Seekers
- Activists & Satirists

Each tag included a clear, simple image with a small blurb about an alum who exemplifies that description. On the Movement Leaders panel, I saw a bunch of asparagus, and "Alice Waters, '67. Acclaimed chef and pioneer behind the worldwide movement to eat local, organic foods." On the Friend Seekers panel, I saw a screenshot of Tom's MySpace page with 201,904,463 friends. It read, "Tom Anderson, '98. Cofounder and president of MySpace.com and first friend to every user." (Remember this was 2007 and MySpace was still relatively popular then.)

The ten images represent a great diversity in alumni in age, gender, ethnicity, and subject area. They are chefs, writers, teachers, scientists, programmers, inventers, cartoonists, and athletes who all have had a profound impact on American culture. Real people, cool people.

On the donation form and envelope, the appeal closes with these simple phrases that say it all to the alumni would-be donors: "Cal alumni are changing the world. Won't YOU champion the next generation of innovators?" followed by "Thanks for being who you are. We appreciate your generosity."

With the fundraising letters I had received before, my internal dialogue went something like, "Sheesh, these old guys are really smart. I don't understand what they are talking about. Did I actually graduate from Cal?" With this new piece, the internal dialogue went like this: "Wow, I went to the same school as these creative, independent firebrands. I'm one of them. I want to support Cal because it nurtures and graduates innovative, free-thinking people like me." I got out my credit card and made a $50 donation.

It's worth noting, however, that I didn't give again. The direct mail that I've received following that particular example seems to have reverted back to focusing on lofty academics that I can't relate to.

THE POWER OF LOGIC, REASON, AND STATISTICS

If you stopped reading this chapter now, you might believe that there is no room for reason or statistics in your nonprofit marketing. But you'd be wrong. Remember, most people make decisions based on emotion, then rationalize or justify those decisions with reason. People decide which charities to support based on an emotional response to the cause, but if you ask them later to explain why they chose that charity, they will often rattle off a list of logical, fact-based reasons. This isn't unique to philanthropy – this basic process of emotion driving decision making and reason justifying those emotions happens in all aspects of our lives. This means that there's definitely a role for statistics in your marketing, but you have to be smart about how you use them. You want facts and statistics to be easily understood and memorable, so that your supporters can recall them later, when explaining to friends and family why they are so generous to your cause.

People have a hard time understanding really big numbers, whether you are talking about millions of people, miles, or hours. The difference between 4,000 people dying and 40,000 people dying is hard for the brain to comprehend. It's just a whole lot of people dying. If the number is overwhelming, then so is the situation, which makes your supporters turn away. They won't be moved by the big number, nor will they remember it, unless you provide some kind of context to make the number real to them.

The Frameworks Institute, which looks at various ways to frame the way we talk about social issues, suggests that nonprofits too often use really big numbers to emphasize the magnitude of a problem or crisis and then end up using small numbers when talking about solutions, leaving supporters with a sense of futility.[5] They recommend using "social math" instead, which blends numbers into stories using analogies. Instead of talking about six tons of toxins being emitted into the air each day, for example, talk about 25 balloons full of toxic pollutants for each schoolchild in town.

Do be careful about the analogies you use. Just because you make the number smaller doesn't mean it will be any easier to understand. The social math needs to make sense in the context of your target community's day-to-day lives. It's also easy to lose sight of the original data once you turn statistics into stories. When you use social math, make sure you can always go back to the original numbers.

DOG PARKS: WHO CARES DURING A RECESSION?

I recall serving as a guest expert in an online chat about nonprofit marketing hosted by the *Chronicle of Philanthropy*. A community organization that was trying to start a dog park wanted to know how it could create compelling messages that would grab prospective supporters when it was competing against so many other causes that were much more directly related to desperate human needs, particularly during a recession.

My advice was to stop trying to compete directly on the basis of need, because it would be a losing battle. Instead, I encouraged the dog park advocates to look at other cultural trends and hot topics that people were captivated by and to use those to make their messages meaningful. Take the cultural shifts that often run parallel to recessions or troubled times: people focusing more on what's really important to them and what brings about genuine quality of life. It's all about family and friends, and dogs are both family *and* friends. I encouraged them to talk about the comfort and security that dogs give both kids and seniors, two perennially popular demographics. To step it up a notch, I suggested they try to find families of soldiers on deployment with kids and dogs left behind, or to find neighbors keeping dogs for soldiers at war, because the impact of the wars in Iraq and Afghanistan on military families also attracts media attention.

Connecting your cause to societal trends and media headlines is a powerful way to tweak your message so it gets more attention.

THE POWER OF A CLEAR CALL TO ACTION

Most of the content you create should end with some kind of call to action or next step. What do you want your readers to do next now that they've read your newsletter? Surely not just delete it or recycle it and move on with their day? Calls to action can be very forceful and direct (for example, volunteer today, donate now, register) or more suggestive and lighter in tone (for example, learn more, tell a friend).

The more time or money you request – the bigger investment you are asking someone to make in you – the more specific your call to action should be. Don't ask people to donate to your cause in the abstract. Explain where the money is going or how the volunteer's time will be used. If a donation is paying for salaries or overhead, talk about what those people actually do with their time and what results from that. What will be accomplished with my donation? That's what your supporters want to know.

You can also use engaging calls to action that build awareness, interaction, and participation. Here are several that work well in the nonprofit sector:

- Learn the signs
- Take the pledge
- Tell someone else to do something (like tell your Senator to vote No)
- Share your story or photo or experience
- Ask a question
- Encourage someone else (like write a letter to a first-time summer camper)
- Take a quiz
- Join the community
- Take the challenge

Create a Powerful Message: What Do You Want to Say? **85**

CHOOSING MESSAGES THAT APPEAL TO YOUR TARGET COMMUNITY

Which of these elements should you incorporate into your message for your specific campaign? It all depends on your community and what you think is most likely to move them. At this stage, it sometimes helps to think of your target community as incredibly selfish people. Of course, the opposite is true. Many of your supporters are extremely generous human beings. But when creating messages about your programs, services, or campaigns, you have to make it all about them – your target community. Appeal not to *your* needs or even the needs of the people you serve, but to the values and needs of your community groups and personas. Make it worth their time.

In nonprofit marketing and especially in fundraising, that means acknowledging the need of your supporters to feel like they are personally making a genuine difference in the life of someone else when they contribute time, money, or influence to your cause. You have to get beyond the indifference to the masses that people naturally feel when confronted with famine or thousands of stranded starfish. Instead, empower them, through your messaging, to be the old man who is willing to make a difference for those starfish, one by one, by appealing to whatever their particular interests and values may be.

Once you have identified your target community and you know who you need to talk to, how do you decide what to say to them? You need to find the intersection between what you want your community to know and do with what they really care about, which may or may not be directly related to your cause.

You do that by describing your program and your call to action in ways that appeal to their values. In commercial marketing terms, you are converting the features of your product into benefits. Seatbelts and airbags in a car are safety features. Not dying in a car accident is a benefit. Red paint and shiny chrome on a sports car are features; feeling powerful and desirable as you drive that car are the benefits.

For nonprofits, converting the features of your good cause into benefits for your supporters often means looking for the emotional payback that your supporters get for giving time or money to your organization or for following through on whatever action you are asking them to take. It's called the benefit exchange. What's in it for them? Do the members of your target community, after absorbing your message and following through on whatever call to action you've requested, get to feel effective, appreciated, powerful, included, heard, validated, relieved, or some other highly valued emotion?

EXAMPLE: MATCHING MESSAGES TO PERSONAS' VALUES

Let's return to our community center example, in which we are trying to market our organization to new volunteers. How can we create messages that match the values of the four personas we created: Anna, Jessica, John, and Miguel?

Anna is our retired person who values predictability. She'd prefer specific, recurring tasks that can be accomplished in a set amount of time. She wants to come in, know what she's doing, get it done, and come back the same time next week. Our messaging to her should make clear that these kinds of set volunteer opportunities are available. She also wants to feel appreciated, so personal thank-you notes from organizational leaders as well as from the people the program helps will work well for her.

For our single mom, Jessica, convenient résumé-building opportunities are going to be most attractive. We need to market to her volunteer tasks that are going to let her stretch herself some, but that also offer some flexibility because of her busy schedule. Wouldn't it be great if we offered something fun for her kids to do while she volunteered? We need to show her that she can improve the lives of others while growing as a professional and as a provider for her family too.

For our well-off businessman, John, we'll be more successful if we emphasize that we have many choices for him and he has control over his volunteer experience. We also want to emphasize how his talents are going to produce real results within the community, so we'll back up the options we provide with data on the results he can expect. He'll enjoy meeting the people who benefit from his volunteer time.

Our college student, Miguel, will be more interested in short-term group activities where friends can volunteer together. We might incorporate a social aspect as well, such as buying pizza for volunteers after the center closes for the day. We might encourage and empower the teens to organize and plan their volunteer activities themselves.

Even though all four of these volunteers may end up performing similar tasks in our community center, these four personas want quite different things out of the experience. If our marketing understands and reflects that, we'll be more successful in recruiting them and ultimately more successful in implementing our mission. Making sure that volunteers understand the real impact that they are having on the lives of specific individuals at the community center would round out marketing to these people.

Now let's say that after looking at our list of longtime donors, we realize that a significant percentage of them volunteered for us at some point. Therefore, we want to create a marketing plan that uses the same four personas we developed for our volunteers group, but now we'll look at ways to motivate them to donate money instead of time. How will their values affect our fundraising messages?

Anna is a retired business owner and is accustomed to public recognition. Leaving a legacy is important to her. That tells us that she might be interested in a planned giving option, such as including the community center in her estate plans. She may also be interested in some naming opportunities, whereby we will put her and her husband's names on an item in the center or name a program after them.

Our single mom, Jessica, has two small children and is unlikely to be interested in talking about estate planning with us. She might, however, be willing to consider a small monthly gift, so explaining the convenience of a monthly automated credit card charge or checking account deduction could work. She's also likely to be a good candidate for active fundraising events, particularly those she could do with her children, like a walk-a-thon. We could also encourage her to ask her church or other service clubs to raise money for the center.

Businessman John likes to have control over his philanthropy, so being clear that he can decide exactly which programs to fund will be important. We also need to ensure that we report back clearly and regularly on the successes that his generous giving produces at the center.

For our young idealist, Miguel, giving money at all may be difficult, so we need to make it easy. Fun events like dance-a-thons could work, and monthly giving at a modest level, even just $5 per month, could work too, as could donating occasionally through his mobile phone via a mobile giving campaign that adds the donation to his phone bill.

CONCLUSION: EVEN THE RELIEF WORKERS WANT TO SAVE THE DARFUR PUPPY

Shortly after Nicholas Kristof's column about the Darfur puppy was published, he received an email from an American relief worker who had actually saved a

Darfur puppy.[6] The aid worker admitted to feeling "slightly ridiculous" about sneaking the weeks-old puppy onto a plane to Khartoum and eventually back to the United States. The Sudan-born dog now lives a happy American life, complete with dog walker, naps on the couch, and romps through the park. Here's how the aid worker described the aftermath of this decision to Kristof:

> I also felt guilty, and still do, that I did so much to save a puppy from Darfur, but not enough to save its people. In that sense, I'm afraid I have a classic case of "psychic numbing," especially after living in Sudan. My only feeble defense is the immediacy of my action – the instant satisfaction I received from saving a life (even a dog's), and the joy I have from watching her grow up.

Even someone who more completely understands the suffering of thousands is still moved by power of saving the one.

Spread Your Message Further by Telling Great Stories

Kelly Nutty, the director of development at Foundations Health & Wholeness, which provides mental health and foster care services, had to find a way to tell stories that still complied with HIPAA (health care privacy rules) and other confidentiality regulations. She started by first explaining to program staff what she did as a fundraiser and why stories were so important. Next, she worked on making it easier for the therapists to work with her. "Asking therapists and social workers to tell me a story isn't effective. It's hard for them to encapsulate the therapeutic process into a powerful story for a donor," said Kelly. Instead, Kelly asks for what she calls nuggets.

"I often post a question on easel paper outside of my office door like 'What do clients say is their biggest barrier to counseling?' or 'What do they say after coming to counseling?' During meetings, I also listen quietly as therapists talk about their clinical struggles," said Kelly. With those nuggets, she can then follow up individually to get exactly the details she needs to tell the story in a way that works in fundraising, changing identifying information as needed.

Kelly also follows up with therapists when the stories they helped create secure a grant or when she gets feedback from donors. "Therapists enjoy hearing that their story made an impact in the community," said Kelly. She also often gives small incentives to therapists for their stories, including cute postcards, little stickers, and other items. "At this point, we've created a storytelling community at our organization between development and program teams. Therapists now seek me out to tell me stories. They understand the power of stories to help us connect with our community, and reduce stigma and fear regarding mental health care," said Kelly. Storytelling isn't just about fundraising anymore, but about engaging the community on mental health issues, too.

Why is storytelling such an incredibly effective form of messaging for nonprofits? Consider my favorite definition from Richard Maxwell and Robert Dickman in their book, *The Elements of Persuasion*:

> A story is a fact, wrapped in an emotion that compels us to take an action that transforms our world.[1]

Nonprofits are all about getting people to take actions that transform our world! So, let's get to wrapping our facts in those emotions.

Telling stories about your cause works so well because, as Chip Heath and Dan Heath – authors of *Made to Stick* (a book I highly recommend to nonprofit communicators) – would say, stories are sticky. They are easier to remember than statistics, making it more likely that our friends will share the story with their friends, creating free word-of-mouth marketing. Stories also help us put a human face on the numbers behind the need, which is essential in fundraising. As the Heath brothers say, stories work because they provide both *simulation*, which is the knowledge about how to act, and *inspiration*, which is the motivation to act.

ADD "STORYTELLER" TO YOUR JOB DESCRIPTION

If storytelling seems intimidating, relax. You don't have to be Shakespeare, some colorful character reading at a children's library, or someone who goes away for long writing retreats.

Good nonprofit marketing stories come in all shapes and sizes. Take the Doritos bag I spotted on my kitchen counter one day. On the back of the bag was this story:

> Divine [Bradley] noticed a lack of resources for the kids growing up in his rough Brooklyn neighborhood, so he brought the problem home with him, literally. At 17, he converted his basement into a community center to give teens in his neighborhood something they sorely needed: options. Divine's organization, Team Revolution, now provides career and financial literacy training. His workshops empower kids to take charge of their lives. The revolution has begun.

It's a great little nonprofit story on the back of a Doritos bag. If nonprofit storytelling works there, you can use your stories anywhere.

You have plenty of material – all nonprofits do. Nonprofits are sitting on a gold mine of stories. You are trying to bring about important changes in people's lives and in the way the world looks, thinks, and works. Anytime you seek change, you invite conflict, and conflict always makes for a great story! Your challenge is to know how to spot those rough nuggets of gold and to polish them up into stories that you can use in your communications and marketing to connect more effectively with potential and current supporters.

Made to Stick identifies three story plots considered to be the most inspirational: the *challenge plot*, the *creativity plot*, and the *connection plot*. I've reviewed hundreds of nonprofit stories and broken down the elements of these three plotlines in detail, so you can understand how to use them, even if you don't believe storytelling comes to you naturally. Keep in mind that mixing and matching elements from the three plots is perfectly fine. For example, you'll often see elements of a challenge plot in a creativity plot story and vice versa.

TELL STORIES WITH THE CHALLENGE PLOT

The challenge plot is the most recognizable plotline, and that's because virtually every Hollywood movie uses it. To mix a few metaphors, these are the classic American stories of the underdog who, against all odds, goes from rags to riches. These stories inspire us to act and to get involved. They appeal to our courage and our strength, and they give us confidence that what we're trying to do really will work. These stories are very empowering for your donors and your volunteers.

The challenge plot follows the classic three-act structure. In Act I, we learn about our protagonist, who should be an individual rather than a group of people. We get some details about their situation and goals. We want to know this is a real person you're talking about, so provide some details about the setting, such as where the person is living, what month and year it is, and so on. We have to understand where this person is headed, or wants to be headed, and get a sense for the barriers that stand in the way.

Here's a simple example that could come from thousands of social service agencies: *A 16-year-old boy named James leaves home in Los Angeles because his drug-addicted mother beats him and hasn't been to a grocery store in months. But living on the streets is tough, and James resorts to shoplifting and mugging people to stay alive.* We can visualize our protagonist in our mind's eye. We understand that he wants a better life than the one his mother is providing, but he's having a hard time on his own.

In Act II, obstacles and conflict appear. The protagonist may overcome some of the smaller obstacles in his way, but we eventually see him falling to a low, and we aren't sure how the story will turn out. The tension mounts. It looks as though a villainous someone or something may prevent our hero from reaching his goals.

Back to our story: *James is arrested and released several times, and after a few months on his own, he decides that life locked up would be easier than life on the streets. In the system, you still have to fight to protect yourself, but at least you get three hots and a cot. He secretly wishes sometimes that he'd get caught doing something serious enough to really get sent away. Then at least he wouldn't have to worry about food or where he was going to sleep that night.*

We see our character reaching a terrible low: this young man now believes that being incarcerated is his best option. The unspoken villain is a society that lets young people like James fall through the cracks and picks them up only long enough to put them in the penal system.

Finally, in Act III, the action peaks. The final obstacle is overcome, and we get the big payoff: the protagonist reaches his goals. We see how this person persevered and triumphed. Close strongly, with a great result. We want to really see the protagonist achieve their goals, with a hopeful outlook for the future.

Here's how our story ends: *Marcus, a Hope House counselor who 10 years earlier had been in much the same situation as James, sees the young man trying to shoplift food one day. He offers to buy the kid lunch, then explains that Hope House is a transitional living center that can help James get off the street, allowing him to get his GED and find a job so that he can support himself, legally. "The people at Hope House believed in me and gave me a second chance at a real life. That's all I really needed," says James.*

Did you notice where the nonprofit in our story came in? In Act III, as a supporting character. The story is still about the protagonist, and it ends with his success. The best challenge plot stories are not about your nonprofit but about someone you are serving. Go back to your mission statement: Why do you exist and who do you serve? Those people and their problems are the basis of Acts I and II. Although human service agencies will have the easiest time with this plot, all nonprofits can use it. Make the story about the people who will be impacted by your work or your partnerships, even if you don't work directly with those people.

TELL STORIES WITH THE CREATIVITY PLOT

Creativity plots are about those big "Aha!" moments in which we reach a breakthrough that solves a nagging problem. They can also be "What if?" stories that encourage people to think about old problems in entirely new and creative ways. If your organization is advocating a different kind of approach to a well-understood problem or talks a lot about "thinking outside the box," the creativity plot will work well for you.

Creativity plots start with a well-understood problem and a typical, commonplace response to that problem that just doesn't work. Let's look at an excerpt from the story behind the founding of Heifer International, as told on their website, as an example of a classic creativity plot.

> A farmer named Dan West was ladling out rations of milk to hungry children during the Spanish Civil War when it hit him. "These children don't need a cup. They need a cow." West, who was serving as a Church of the Brethren relief worker, was forced to decide who would receive the limited rations and who wouldn't. This kind of aid, he knew, would never be enough.

The well-understood problem is clear: starving children. The old approach that just isn't working is clear too: rations dispensed in food lines.

The second half of the creativity plot is the new, innovative approach to the old problem – and the promise it holds for creating a new reality. In many of these stories, the new approach has yet to be fully proven. Test runs and theories are fine, but it's important to close with the big vision of the problem solved, just like in the challenge plot where you need to close with the individual's triumph.

The Heifer International story continues:

> West returned home to form Heifers for Relief, dedicated to ending hunger permanently by providing families with livestock and training so they could be spared the indignity of depending on others to feed their children . . . This simple idea of giving families a source of food, rather than short-term relief, caught on and has continued

for over 60 years. Since 1944, Heifer has helped 8.5 million people in more than 125 countries.

Here we see the creative solution: Don't give them a cup of milk, give them the cow that's going to produce over and over. Give heifers, female livestock, that will produce offspring that can be shared with others in the community. It's an entirely new way of fighting an old problem, and it's now spread worldwide. It's a classic creativity plot.

TELL STORIES WITH THE CONNECTION PLOT

Connection plots are what you might call bridging-the-gap stories because they are often about unlikely connections. These stories are often about a small, seemingly inconsequential event with a surprise twist that ends up revealing some kind of universal truth or lesson. They can also make you think, "There but for the grace of God go I." Stories with a connection plot may be the hardest of the three to write, but they are also the most emotionally powerful. These stories, when done well, can work wonders in fundraising letters.

Take a look at this blog post from ReSurge International (formerly Interplast), a nonprofit that performs surgeries on cleft palate defects and burn injuries in developing countries. It's one of my favorite connection plot stories of all time. It's written in the voice of Janet Volpe, one of the doctors on the trip.

> This is Van Canh with his wife and 9-month-old daughter, Thi Sang. Thi Sang was born with a cleft lip, like her father. When Van Canh heard that Interplast was coming to Cao Lanh, he and his wife decided, despite financial hardship, to leave their family store for the day and make the two-hour bus journey to our clinic day to have their daughter evaluated. Fourteen years ago, Interplast operated on clefts on both sides of Van Canh's mouth. He had been told he would need a revision in the future, but because of work and family commitments, he had never been able to make it back for the revision. As our team evaluated Thi Sang, we asked Van Canh if he'd like to have his clefts revised during our stay. He and his wife were overjoyed that we would consider this for him. At the age of 26 years, he told us he thought he was too old for Interplast to want to perform another surgery on him, and had no money to have the revision

performed locally. We scheduled the surgeries one day apart, and this photo was taken at the time of discharge from the hospital. Van Canh had brought chewing gum from his store; just before going home, he gave each member of our team a stick as a token of appreciation. I taped my Wrigley's Doublemint wrapper in my journal and will always remember this kind and grateful family.

Connection plots often start with a small specific situation or event that may not be particularly noteworthy on its own. But as the story progresses, a connection to a greater, universal human experience is revealed. This often comes through a surprise, a discovery, or some kind of epiphany. We see connections between the characters in these stories, but also between the person listening to the story and the people in it.

In the story about Van Canh, the small, specific situation was the father bringing his daughter in for the surgery. The nonprofit could have written this up focusing on the little girl, and it could have been a nice success story that demonstrates the work they do. But then we get the twist: the father went through this same experience as a child, but still needed another surgery. Now they are offering to perform his surgery too.

The human connection is about gratitude. The father giving all he could – a stick of gum – was all the doctor needed to feel the family's appreciation. The doctor was so touched that she kept her gum wrapper, reminding her to be grateful for everything she has, and reminding us of the same thing as we read the story.

USE THE SIX QUALITIES OF A GOOD NONPROFIT MARKETING STORY

You need more than a good plot for a story to work in nonprofit marketing. Strive for these six qualities in your stories.

Short. Take only as long to tell the story as you really need to. If you are telling a story online, try for 500 words or less. If you are producing a video, no more than two minutes is ideal.

Straightforward. Be clear and straightforward. Don't try to do too much. Avoid going off on tangents, even if they seem interesting, because they will detract from the main reason you are telling the story.

Personal. Your stories should be about specific people, not general stand-ins for a larger population. Make it personal. Limit the number of people in the story. In the connection plot example, we don't learn much about the doctor, other than her narrative voice and her reaction to the stick of gum. Nor do we hear much at all about the wife or the daughter. The story is primarily about the father, and it focuses our attention on the connections with him.

Authentic. We connect with stories that ring true. We don't want to hear stories about impossibly perfect people. We hate those people! We want to hear about the people who are like us, human and imperfect, making mistakes and learning from those mistakes. We want to hear about real people, even if their names or other identifying characteristics are changed to protect their privacy.

Includes conflict or imperfections. Conflict and imperfections are what bring stories to life and make us care about how they turn out. That sometimes means providing unflattering details about clients. If you work in social services, your stories may include drug abuse and criminal behavior. But we have to understand the complicated and rough histories in order to see how amazing the transformation of the person in the story truly is.

Ends with a message. Although storytelling is a wonderful tool for nonprofit marketing, it works only when you have a specific goal in mind. Make sure that the message of your story is clear. You don't necessarily need to say, "And this story means that . . ." The story itself should make that clear. Your readers or listeners should understand what they are supposed to be feeling and what they are supposed to do next.

FIND FRESH STORY IDEAS

When the blank computer screen is staring back at you, knowing *what* to write about (or talk about on a podcast or video) can be challenging, even if you understand *how* to write a story using one of the three plots we reviewed. Here are my 10 favorite sources of story ideas for nonprofit communicators. Keep in mind that these are places to look for inspiration and story ideas, not necessarily for the story content itself. Don't violate anyone's copyrights by using their content without permission.

1. *The receptionist's desk.* Ask whoever answers your organization's main phone number for the top three questions callers ask, then turn the answers into stories for your newsletter, blog, and other messaging.

2. *Your clients' and supporters' lives.* Ask the people your organization helps about what's happening in their lives right now, what questions they are pondering, or what decisions they are making. Ask some of your supporters the same thing. Ask them to explain what their situation was like before working with your organization and what it's like now. You can also survey your donors, clients, or members about the issues they care about.

3. *Your newsletter or blog archives.* What did you write about this time last year? Can you freshen up an old article or provide a timely update on something you've covered before?

4. *The headlines.* Look at the last week's worth of headlines from your local newspaper or the website of your favorite national TV news network or magazine. What issues are they covering and how are those news items related to your work?

5. *Your calendar.* Think about hooks tied into holidays and other special days on the calendar. There are hundreds of specially designated weeks and months. For example, June is Adopt a Shelter Cat Month, National Iced Tea Month, and Rebuild Your Life Month. Chase's Calendar of Events is the ultimate source for all such occasions, but you can find many lists free online.

6. *Your web stats.* Look at your website statistics and you'll find what keywords people are typing into search engines before they direct traffic to your website. Take those phrases and write detailed articles on those topics.

7. *News aggregators.* Go to your favorite mainstream or trade news source and look for trends.

8. *Event programs.* See who's talking about what at various conferences, workshops, and webinars related to your work. Ask to interview those experts or ask whether they'd like to submit a guest post.

9. *Twitter trends.* See what hashtags are trending on Twitter. Maybe you can connect something in your work to a popular hashtag.

10. *Google search trends.* Google publishes its top trending searches. Again, can you connect the dots between a hot search trend and something in your own work?

INTERVIEW YOUR SUPPORTERS FOR PROFILES AND STORIES

Nonprofit stories often take the form of personal profiles of people associated with the organization. You'll often find them under headings like Volunteer Spotlight, Friends of [Your Issue], and Meet the Board. Nonprofits also use profiles to put a specific human face on their programs, accomplishments, needs, and advocacy positions.

Every good profile starts with an interview. Here are 10 tips I've learned after writing many a profile over the years:

1. *Don't ask for information you can easily get elsewhere.* Do your homework. Don't ask your board chair where she works or what her title is. Don't ask a donor how much he has given your organization. You should already have that information. It's OK to ask people to *confirm* the spelling of their names or if the total amount donated over several years sounds right to them, but this should be presented as quick fact-checking, not as part of the interview.

2. *Don't fall into Tedious Bio Syndrome.* It's the narrative equivalent of a résumé. Or worse, you start when they were born. Profiles that start that way are total snoozers, and so are the interviews themselves.

3. *Be flexible about the format.* You can get the information you need whether you conduct the interview in person, over the phone, or via email. I find it's actually easier to take good notes while interviewing over the phone, rather than in person, because I don't have to worry about maintaining eye contact, and I can type much faster than I can write. Invest in a good, comfortable headset for hands-free phone conversations. People who are a bit nervous about being interviewed often prefer email, because it gives them time to mull over their answers.

4. *Prepare a list of questions but be willing to stray from it.* Come up with some good questions to get the conversation going, but don't be afraid to ask new questions or take the interview in a different direction, as long as you are getting good details and quotes. Listen for intriguing details or good sound bites and follow them.

5. *Ask open-ended questions that contain emotional words.* Fact-filled profiles simply aren't as interesting as those full of feeling and emotion. To

get your subject to provide you with good anecdotes and quotes, ask questions that are variations on "How did that make you feel?" Try questions like "What has surprised you most about . . . ?" "What upsets you most about . . . ?" and "What do you remember most about . . . ?"

6. *Don't be a gushing fan.* It's fine if you admire the person you are talking to, but don't interview them as a fan. You'll end up writing the worst kind of profile: the Obvious Kiss-Up. Be nice to your VIPs, but don't overdo it.

7. *If you are writing the story with a specific purpose in mind, ask some leading questions.* For example, if you are profiling Mrs. Smith because she put your nonprofit in her will, and you want to encourage others to do the same, you need to ask Mrs. Smith some leading questions to elicit the right kind of quotes. For example, you might ask, "Why did you select our nonprofit specifically when you could have left your gift to any group?" and "How did you feel after you made the decision?" Asking donors about the kind of legacy they want to leave behind can also work well.

8. *Don't go astray with entertaining but irrelevant stories.* Sometimes you'll interview someone who loves to talk and tell you funny stories about all of their friends. Although it might be a very entertaining conversation for both of you, you will end up with little that you can use in your profile. Warming up to each other with stories about wild adventures abroad are fine, but then steer the conversation back to the subject of the profile.

9. *Give the interviewee control over the content.* This is not hard news or "gotcha" journalism. You are profiling people because you care about them and because they care about your cause. Ask whether your profile subject would like to see the story you write before it is published (most will say yes). Give them a few days to get back to you with any changes they feel are important. This ensures not only that you have your facts straight, but also that your supporters are pleased with the way they are portrayed in your communications.

10. *Follow up within a few days with any additional questions.* Don't wait too long after your original interview to write the profile. That way you can quickly follow up with additional questions while the conversation is still fresh in both of your minds.

PROTECT THE PRIVACY OF THE PEOPLE IN YOUR STORIES

Like Kelly at the beginning of this chapter, many nonprofits must wrangle with legal and ethical issues when talking about the people they serve. But don't use confidentiality requirements as an excuse for avoiding storytelling. You can approach this challenge in several different ways.

Get permission. Simply ask the person if it's OK to tell his or her story, or if you need something more formal (good for potentially controversial or otherwise touchy topics), ask the person to sign a release. You can find sample release language by searching online for "story release form" or "model release form." Write the story, complete with the level of detail you would like to share. Let the subject of the story read it and make any desired edits. When you explain how you'll be using the story to build support for your agency, many people are not only flattered but also pleased to be able to give back in this way.

Change identifying details. You can change elements of the story that are not central to it in order to protect someone's identity. You can change the person's name, location, age, and other demographics that are irrelevant to the outcome of the story.

Create a composite. You can combine elements of more than one person's story into a new fictional character. However, be careful not to present this person as a real human being. Instead, open your story with language like, "Imagine if you were a . . ." or "What if . . ." By using this approach, you are making the story more about the listeners or readers and asking your community to put themselves in the shoes of someone else. Ensure that your composite still rings true and sounds as if it could be a real person in your community, even if it isn't.

INCORPORATE STORIES INTO YOUR COMMUNICATIONS

Here are 10 specific ways you can use stories in your day-to-day communications:

1. *Include a story about a real person in every speech you give.* Talking to potential volunteers? Tell a story or two about real volunteers and the difference they are making in the lives of others.

2. *Turn a story into a how-to article for your newsletter.* Using the first person ("How I . . ."), have someone on your staff, a board member, or a volunteer

explain how to do something, based on that person's own experience in learning how to do it.

3. *Include testimonials in your event marketing.* Ask people who attended your workshop to provide testimonials about how they personally used what they learned at the event in their own work.

4. *Single out one person you are helping in your next fundraising appeal letter.* Instead of talking broadly about the need for low-cost childcare in your community, talk about the plight of just one single mom.

5. *Use serial storytelling on a campaign blog.* Hook in readers with frequent updates about a particular person, animal, or item. Environmental and humane groups use this tactic effectively all the time (such as tracking a particular whale's journey – "Will he evade the evil whale hunters?" – or profiling a dog that has been badly abused, but is now on the mend after being rescued – "Will she live? And walk again?").

6. *Give each board member at least one good story to use.* Your board members should be advocating for your organization at all times. Give them real stories they can use that will put your organization in a good light with potential donors, volunteers, community decision makers, and so on. Make time on your next board meeting agenda to hear stories and to practice telling them.

7. *Lead your next press release with a story.* The media loves real stories, so use them as angles in your press releases. If you can make the real person in the story available for interviews, that's even better.

8. *Incorporate a story into a training session.* Who do you train? Volunteers, new staff, community members, others in your field? Incorporate a good story into your next training session.

9. *Add stories to your annual report.* They can take the form of personal profiles, first-person accounts, or short testimonials, but include stories about real people in your annual report to reinforce the narrative about your accomplishments and activities.

10. *Rotate stories on your website home page.* Collect stories about specific people related to your organization and rotate them on your home page.

CONCLUSION: STORIES ARE A NONPROFIT'S GOLD MINE

If you are not using storytelling as an essential element in your nonprofit marketing and communications, you are robbing yourself of one of the most effective tools available to you.

"No matter whether I'm working on a newsletter or being interviewed by a reporter, I always think 'Tell a story,'" said Lane Phalen, a former board member of the TAILS Humane Society in DeKalb, Illinois. "Why do we need donations to build an outdoor fence for dogs? Chip, a retriever mix, needs to stretch his legs to relieve energy so he can remain in his kennel for the other twenty-three hours of the day. Why do we need extra donations to pay medical bills? Missy, a black cat left at our doorstep, had a gnarled and broken leg that was so bad, we had to amputate it. But then we got her back in good health and found a home for her." Telling stories makes the needs and the successes of your organization real to your supporters.

Nonprofits are story gold mines. You now know the elements of three inspirational plotlines that work well for nonprofits, where to look for stories, and where to use them. Take the time to do some mining. Stop and look for those rough rocks and polish them up into beautiful gems. Wear them yourself and share them with others every day.

Adopt an Attitude of Gratitude

My sister and business partner, Kristina, was avoiding work one day and found herself deep down one of those Wikipedia rabbit holes she so often finds herself in. "I honestly can't remember if I was chasing true crime stories, tracing the British monarchy, or checking out the plots to books I will never read, but still want to know about," said Kristina. "But it was during a Wikipedia pledge drive and since I spend a lot of time on Wikipedia, I absentmindedly gave $20."

The thank-you email that Kristina immediately received surprised her because it felt so personal and genuine. It read, in part:

> Dear Kristina,
>
> I feel so lucky to be the person to thank you for your $20 gift on behalf of a world of people seeking free knowledge.
>
> I used to try to guess what motivated you to give, but the longer I do this work, the more I realize I can't put your curiosity in a box. There is no one singular experience of Wikipedia. Curiosity is as diverse as we all are, and it looks a little different for each of us.
>
> When you use Wikipedia next, I hope you feel that it belongs to you. Because without you, and without the millions of people who come back to us every day, we would be nothing.
>
> Thank you for giving Wikipedia shape, and purpose, and momentum. Thank you for fitting us into your life.
>
> With immense gratitude,
>
> Katherine Maher, Executive Director

Now Kristina works in nonprofit communications. She knows this is an automated letter. She knows the executive director of Wikipedia was not anxiously awaiting her $20, and she knows she is not the only one who received this letter.

Does any of that matter to Kristina? No!

"I only gave $20, but I still got a thank you. A lot of nonprofits only send thank-you letters to donors who have given above a certain amount. I also received this immediately," said Kristina. "I also loved how the email looked like a plain email that any of us would write. And she repeatedly spoke to me as a real person of curiosity and commitment. Because of her thank-you note, I do believe that Wikipedia belongs to me!"

I wish Kristina's experience was universal for all donors and all nonprofits. When you receive a well-written, personal thank-you note, you are more likely to give again and to give even more generously the next time. When you don't get a thank-you note, you remember, and you probably think a little less of the recipient. Kids who want nicer gifts from their grandparents should wise up, and so should nonprofits.

Sending a thank-you note to a supporter is the courteous, appropriate response to a gift of any size or kind, whether it's cash, time, an introduction to an important person, or a tip about an especially helpful resource. But it's also a shrewd marketing and fundraising strategy because it works, and because so few nonprofits do it regularly and do it well. Forget the latest, greatest fundraising success secrets and get back to basics. Adopt an attitude of gratitude and infuse it into your messaging.

DONORS ARE TESTING NONPROFITS, AND NONPROFITS ARE FAILING

In numerous experiments run by various nonprofit professionals, including several I've run myself, nonprofits are failing miserably at creating compelling thank-you letters and other forms of gratitude messaging.

Donors often start their relationship with nonprofits with small gifts, like Kristina's $20, not because they can't afford more, but because they are a bit uncertain or are giving spontaneously and small gifts are comfortable to make in an instant. They want to see how you will use the money and how results will be communicated back to them. They want to feel like part of the solution, not part of an ATM. Yet many studies and lagging donor rates tell us that many organizations are failing to meet these expectations.

Penelope Burk's research shows that donors want something quite simple: a prompt, meaningful thank-you letter and additional communication that explains how the donation was used. That's it. Eighty percent of donors say that would convince them to make that second gift.

And yet the typical thank-you note that many nonprofits send out is more like a transaction receipt than a warm, personalized acknowledgment of generosity, which reinforces the ATM mentality that supporters fear. Donors are inspired to give by their hearts and their souls, and you need to give them thank-you letters that speak to their hearts and their souls, not to their checkbook.

Even if you send thank-you letters out now, odds are good that they won't stand out in your donors' minds. That's because most of these letters look and sound the same. Most thank-you letters start out the same way: "On behalf of . . ." or "Thank you for your gift of . . ." Although starting a thank-you letter that way isn't bad per se, it is predictable and tired.

Very few thank-you letters specify how the gift will be used, leaving the donor to wonder what kind of difference the gift will make if any at all. We also see thank-you notes that are plain depressing. They emphasize how much need is still out there without making donors feel good about what they have already done with their first gift. Rather than inspiring people to give more, this approach brings people down and makes them question whether their investment in your nonprofit was a wise one.

A 2018 study by Professor Jen Shang, Professor Adrian Sargeant, Kathryn Carpenter, and Harriet Day of the Philanthropy Centre and Plymouth University reveals more insights into how donors should be thanked.[1]

Early in the relationship, according to the study, you should focus on sharing with the donor the difference their gift has made. When the donor makes many gifts, you can thank them for being the special kind of person that they are and talk about how much the donor means to the charity. Getting this right increases the well-being that the individual experiences and their subsequent giving, the study says.

The study also found that a thank-you can be used strategically in a communications cycle to boost a donor's personal sense of well-being. A thank-you for past giving in advance of a new campaign can significantly increase the value of giving during the campaign by 60 percent. This is one of the many reasons that gratitude campaigns around Thanksgiving often precede annual appeal drives in December.

The experiments conducted by the research team showed that even subtle changes to communications can influence how well donors feel as a result of reading that communication. Based on the experiments, the Philanthropy Centre recommends the following advice.

After people make their first donation, send communications primarily to thank them for the differences their donations have made. After people give more often than the average number of times of supporters in your database, send a letter primarily thanking them for the long-term relationship that they have with specific key stakeholders or personalities in your organization, or for being who they are.

These practices, according to the study, have the potential to increase average donation amount and response rates, as well as how competent donors feel in making a difference, how well they feel their donations allow them to express their beliefs, and how connected they feel they are to the cause they support.

IMPROVE YOUR THANK-YOU NOTES IN SIX STEPS

A good thank-you letter reassures donors that they have made the right decision to invest in your organization. That's how donors see themselves today – as investors in social good. This is especially true for baby boomers and younger generations, who see charitable giving as an investment of themselves in your organization. They expect to see a return on that investment. This is a significant cultural shift. The World War II generation gave out of a sense of duty and responsibility and was more trusting about how the recipient spent the money. Nowadays you need to be clear about your intentions, follow through on them, and communicate that to your supporters. This is also your opportunity to welcome new supporters into a community of others who care about your particular issue. Even if you're not a membership organization per se, you still want to create a sense of belonging to something bigger.

Let's look at several ways to improve your thank-you letters.

Get Them Out Quickly

Ideally you will send out your thank-you letters within 48 hours of receiving the gifts – definitely within one week. If you wait any longer than that, you risk disconnecting your letter from the gift. Keep the conversation alive by responding quickly. It can be time-consuming to write good letters, but you need to make the time, because it's not only the right thing to do but also an investment in your future financial health. I would rather see an organization spending time on creating great thank-you letters than spending time on a newsletter. Put sending your thank-you letters at the top of your communications to-do list.

Personalize Them

Use mail merge to personalize your thank-you letters so you are addressing the person by name and using specific details like the gift amount and any personal designation (such as for memorial gifts in a loved one's name). Avoid "Dear Friend" or "Dear Supporter" if at all possible. The check or credit card the donor used has a real name on it and so should the thank-you letter.

It's also a nice touch to handwrite an additional note on the letter. Nonprofits do this on fundraising solicitations all the time, and it works well on thank-you notes too. Including photos, either in the body of the letter or stuffed in an envelope, will also help personalize the letter. A photo of a client or smiling people making a difference out there in the world will light up your donor's day. Get together a group of people whom your organization helps and take a photo of them holding a big banner that says, "Thank You."

You can also personalize letters by telling stories about the people you serve in the body of the letter. Even though you probably can't say right away that this $50 donation helped James, by telling James's story and how other donations have helped James, your new donor will see the connection between their gift and the types of results they can expect.

Use a More Creative Opening

Forget "On behalf of" or "Thank you for" – start your letters with a more creative and personal opening. Try something like, "You made my day" on one line by itself. Then jump into a story: "Your donation crossed my desk today and . . ." Explain how the money will be used. Or start with, "I have a great story to share with you." Launch right into a success story, then talk about how the donation will create even more happy endings. Starting with something like, "Guess what you've made possible?" is another interesting way to introduce a success story.

Jump right into these stories and save the actual thank-you verbiage for later in the letter. When you get to that point, thank the person for his or her generosity, rather than for the money. You can start with, "I am so thankful for people like you." Don't talk about the money; talk about the person. Giving money is only one way that people can make a difference.

Explain How the Gift Will Be Used

Very quickly but clearly describe a specific program for which the gift will be used. If you are fundraising for specific programs this will be easier than if you are fundraising for general support. But even then, you still need to give supporters a sense for what you're doing with the money. You can use anecdotes as examples for how the money is being spent, or you can assure donors that their gifts are going to "where the need is greatest." The vaguer you are in the thank-you letter about how you are spending the gift, the more specific you should be about it when you will follow up with details about results.

Tell Them What to Expect Next

Start creating a relationship by explaining how you plan to keep the lines of communication open. Tell your donors that you will be adding them to your newsletter list and that they can unsubscribe at any time, should they choose. Most donors are going to be perfectly happy to start getting information from you. Tell them what's going to be in that newsletter, when they can expect it, and what it's going to look like, so they know to look for it. Invite them to learn more about your work by visiting your website or scheduling a tour of your office. Many organizations do special briefings, lunches, or conference calls for their major donors a few times a year, so mention that you'll be inviting them to participate in those too. Also make sure they are aware of volunteer opportunities.

Personalize from the Sender, Too

Just as you are personalizing the "to" part of the letter, you also need to personalize the "from" part. Ideally, the signature is from someone with stature in the organization. Sign your letters in ink, rather than using a digital image. Even if an intern is signing your name, a real signature is better than a computer-generated one on a thank-you note. It shows that you care enough to take the time to do it.

Letters from volunteer leaders to donors can have a big impact, so if you can coordinate with your board members to get the letters out quickly, give it a try. If you can't get them all done that way, that's fine. Have the board members personalize only those thank-you letters that need to go out around the same time as the board meeting. Or ask board members to send a separate handwritten thank-you note or even an email as a follow-up to your "official" thank-you letter.

Phone calls from board members can also be really powerful, as long as you aren't asking for anything else. Simply call to say thank you and to pass on a brief success story or explanation of how the gift will be used.

Letters from clients are another great approach to personalizing the sender. If you work in any kind of human service organization with many clients who benefit from programs funded by individual donations, give this approach a try. According to Penelope Burk's research, 76 percent of donors say that getting a thank-you letter from someone who benefited from a charity's work would be very meaningful to them. Ask your clients to explain in their own words how your organization has changed their lives and to thank the donor for making it all possible.

CREATE THANK-YOU VIDEOS

Videos, in addition to letters, are also a great way to share your gratitude, both individually and collectively. A number of video software companies offer tools that allow you to quickly create a personal video for one donor, where you can thank them by name and then email that video directly to your donor.

But you can also create collective thank-you videos for all of your supporters. Here are five different themes that many nonprofits have used successfully in thank-you videos.

1. *Thanks to You.* In this approach, a narrator shares perhaps a dozen organizational accomplishments that all begin with the phrase "Because of you" or "Thanks to you." For example, you might hear, "Thanks to you, our kids can explore the arts and dance. Thanks to you, kids are getting healthy meals at lunch. Thanks to you, these kids' futures are much brighter."

2. *Because of You, I.* These videos are narrated in the first person usually by several clients or program participants who each add one statement. Like the first theme, they share a variety of accomplishments but follow the same pattern. "Because of you, I can live on my own. Because of you, I feel safe. Because of you, I can take care of myself now."

3. *Holding Thank-You Signs.* These videos usually have an upbeat music soundtrack and we see staff and clients holding up signs, often homemade, with the words "Thank You" on them. These videos are very quick and easy to make.

4. *Multiple Narrators with Message Repetition.* In these videos we see and hear different people repeat the same messaging. They are often reading the same script, and then the individual videos are edited together so each speaker says only a small part of the complete message.

5. *This Is What Gratitude Looks Like.* In these videos, we see the results: usually smiling kids, laughing adults, tail-wagging dogs, or other signals that problems are being solved and there's hope for a better tomorrow.

We've created many playlists of thank-you videos (and other kinds of nonprofit videos too) at youtube.com/nonprofitmarketingguide.

PUBLISH A SHORT ANNUAL REPORT

Even though nonprofit organizations aren't required to produce annual reports as publicly traded companies are, most nonprofit managers recognize the value of producing one. Annual reports can help you demonstrate your accomplishments to current and future donors, cultivate new partnerships, and recognize important people. Think of your annual report as a special kind of thank-you note.

Shorter annual reports are a trend that I have been advocating for years. No one wants to read a 30-page annual report. Try to keep them under 10 pages or go even shorter. We share many examples at NonprofitMarketingGuide.com of annual reports in the form of postcards, infographics, and two-minute videos.

But because annual reports aren't legally required, nonprofits often struggle with what should be included in an annual report and what should be left out. The following 10 tips will help you craft an outstanding nonprofit annual report.

1. *Focus on accomplishments, not activities.* We want to know what you did, but more important, we want to know *why* you did it. What were the results? Why did you spend your time and money the way you did? What difference did it make? Connect the everyday activities of your organization to your mission statement. Don't assume that readers will automatically understand how your activities help you achieve your mission. Connect the dots for them.

2. *Jettison the administrative minutiae.* Getting new desk chairs and new accounting software may be big accomplishments from where you sit at your desk, but they have nothing to do with your mission. Inspire donors with accomplishments related to your mission in your annual report and leave all the administrative items for your board report.

3. *Don't overemphasize fundraising accomplishments.* Donors expect you to raise money, but fundraising accomplishments should not be celebrated in your annual report on the same level as your mission-related accomplishments. Readers are more interested in what you did with the money than how you raised it. Although it is appropriate to include information on how well your fundraising efforts are going, it's best to place this information in the financial section of your report, rather than front and center.

4. *Include photos.* Yes, pictures really are worth a thousand words. Many of the people reading your annual report won't actually read it. Show them what you've been doing with photos. If you don't have a digital camera, get one now. It's also fine to use stock photography to illustrate your work. Enter "royalty free stock photos" in your favorite search engine and you'll find numerous sites.

5. *Write captions that tell your story.* Now that you've got them looking at the photos, tell a story with your captions. Don't just state what's in the photo. Connect the photo to an accomplishment. If people read nothing but the captions in your annual report, they should still get a sense for the good work you did last year.

6. *Include personal profiles.* Donors will be more impressed with real stories about real people than general summaries of your work. Explain what you have accomplished overall, then humanize your statistics with some personal profiles. Highlight how your work helped a specific individual. Share a volunteer's story of how they made a positive difference.

7. *Explain your financials.* Many of your donors won't know how to read a financial statement or won't take the time to read it. Include a paragraph or two that explains in plain language what the tables say. Where does your money come from and how do you spend it? What are your main fundraising strategies? Did you implement any cost-savings measures this year?

8. *If you need space, trim the donor lists, or cut them entirely.* Nonprofits need to strike a balance between using the space in their annual reports to discuss their accomplishments and using it to recognize donors. If as much as half of your annual report is donor lists, you should consider scaling the lists back to make more room for text and photos. In fact, I often advocate that you remove the donor list entirely.

9. *Triple-check your donor lists.* There's no better way to sabotage a future donation than to spell the donor's name wrong in your annual report. If you are uncertain about a name, don't guess. Check it with the donor. Also carefully check the names of government agencies and foundations that gave you grants. The names people call these organizations in conversation are often shorthand for the full legal names that belong in your annual report.

10. *Tell donors how they can help.* Never leave potential supporters hanging, wondering how they can help you. Once you've inspired them with the good works in your annual report, close by telling them how they can help you do more. How can they support you with their money or time? Do you offer planned giving options, for example? Will you accept gifts of stock? Can they use a credit card? Be clear about the best ways to help.

CONCLUSION: STOP MAKING EXCUSES; MAKE THE TIME INSTEAD

When I talk to nonprofits about how important it is to write thank-you notes, I often feel like a nag. Perhaps even you felt nagged reading this chapter! But the reason I'm devoting an entire chapter of this book to them is because responding to the generosity of your supporters with gratitude really is a core element of a successful nonprofit marketing program.

Don't say you don't have the time for something this important. Give higher priority to your thank-you notes than to any other piece of communication you work on. The newsletter doesn't go out, the website doesn't get updated, and your report to your board doesn't get done until you have sent your thank-you letters to your donors. Failing to do so is a sure road to remaining underfunded and understaffed. Following through is the path to even more generosity from your supporters.

chapter TEN

Deliver Your Message: How and Where Are You Going to Say It?

When Hillary Ryan, the director of marketing and communications at the Tacoma Art Museum, started a previous job at a different art museum several years ago, she became responsible for a beautifully designed 40-page quarterly online magazine for members. It had wonderful images, detailed calendar information, and lovely stories.

So why did Hillary head to her boss's office and say they couldn't continue the publication? "After finding out that this particular piece took anywhere from 40–80 hours to create, I wanted to see how it was being used. When checking on the open rates, I found that less than 1 percent of our people were even engaging with this digital magazine," said Hillary.

It was clear: the community the magazine was sent to had no interest in reading the content online.

She discovered that the member magazine used to be a print publication. But when faced with budget cuts, the organization eliminated it and decided instead to put the content online. But they had failed to check to see if that was an option the community wanted.

"As the person now in charge, it was important for me to find some way to bring back the print piece that had connected with museum members," said Hillary.

She restarted the print publication small – just one 11 × 17 sheet folded in half with an inserted calendar that eventually grew to eight pages. Hillary also diversified the content to include not only imagery and articles about art, but content on the artists as people, make-at-home art instructions for families, and coupons for the museum store.

While the amount of time put into the new print publication was about the same as the old digital version, the results were significantly better. It took a few years of trial and error, but Hillary eventually came up with a new print magazine that produced much better engagement than the digital version while also creating useful content she could repurpose into other channels.

"This piece is now seen as a benefit of membership and as a tool for development staff to use during major gift and other solicitations," said Hillary. In addition, because of design and printing deadlines, staff are pushed to make decisions and commit to calendar items. "In the digital space, it was too easy for people to just ask for on-the-fly changes and that created an awful workflow."

As you can see from Hillary's experience, the way you answer the third Quick-and-Dirty Marketing Plan question, "How do we deliver this message to those people?" requires as much care and strategy as deciding who you are talking to and what your message is.

You need to create content by packing your messaging into words and images that will travel to your community's eyes and ears. You'll publish and distribute that content through multiple communications channels, searching for ways to reach your community where they already are.

Let's start by looking at the words, then your visuals, followed by your various communications channels.

THE SEVEN WRITING STYLES FOR NONPROFIT COMMUNICATORS

Different communities and different communications channels demand different writing styles. You wouldn't use the same kind of language when speaking to a classroom of high school students about why they should volunteer for you as you would when addressing a classroom of university faculty about your research needs. The language choices you make for a press release or annual report may or may not work on various social media platforms.

At Nonprofit Marketing Guide, we've identified seven different writing styles that most nonprofit communicators should understand and master over time.

1. News Writing

News writing is straightforward, factual writing found in press releases, reports, and blogs. It covers the five Ws and one H: Who, what, when, where, why, and how. It follows the inverted pyramid style of writing where you share the most newsworthy information right away, followed by the important details, and closing with other general information or background. Note that this is the reverse of how many academic essays or papers are written, where you start with the background information and save your conclusions for the end.

2. Storytelling

Nonprofit storytelling refers to narratives about participants and supporters that include characters, descriptive details, emotions, and plot. Nonprofits use many different formulas for stories. I shared three that I like, along with other storytelling tips, in Chapter 8.

3. Supporter-Centered Copywriting

Supporter-centered or donor-centered copywriting delivers repeated emotional gratification and gratitude to people for their support. It is most often found in appeal letters, donor newsletters, thank-you letter copy, and annual reports. It is nearly always in the second person and effusive in gratitude, e.g. "Because of you, hundreds of children are sleeping safely tonight. Thank you for your unwavering commitment to protecting them."

4. Lifestyle Writing

Lifestyle writing is casual or informal yet engaging content, frequently found online. There's almost always a hook that grabs the reader's attention. It's harder to write than it looks. Lifestyle writing includes popular formats such as how-to articles, advice columns, top 10 lists, and reviews.

5. Thought Leadership

Thought leadership writing includes authoritative and opinionated content that positions the person or organization as an expert and leader. The writing has a clear point of view. It can take many forms, including reports from the front lines, op-ed pieces, and longer manifestos.

6. Microcontent

Microcontent refers to the short but powerful pieces of copy you find in headlines, subject lines, captions, and tweets. When people are skimming content, they read the microcontent first, and may stop there. If the microcontent is compelling enough, they will read into your paragraphs. Some microcontent techniques are timeless, such as asking a question, using a number, and using personal pronouns like *My* and *You*.

7. Conversion Copywriting

Conversion copywriting is persuasive writing that motivates immediate action, including clicking, donating, registering, etc. It always speaks directly to the reader in a short, clear, direct way and is singularly focused on getting the reader to complete a desired action. It answers not only "Why?" but "Why now?" Conversion copywriting should be used around any form or button in your online communications.

Don't bury your well-focused and targeted message in jargon and other stiff language that doesn't connect with your community. Decide on the appropriate writing style then spend time finding the right words to share your messaging with your community.

SUPPORT YOUR WORDS WITH IMAGES

Photography and graphics – both stills and video – can be incredibly powerful in conveying your message. You can use actual images of your organization's activities to show exactly what it is you do and who's doing it for whom. You can visually show problems and solutions. You can also use symbolic imagery to reinforce metaphors you may be using to get your points across (for example, a photo of a seedling to convey early growth or a large old tree to convey enduring strength).

It's best to use your own original photos and video, but when you don't have the right images for your message, consider using stock photography. It's true that many people despise stock photography because much of it looks too polished, posed, generic, or fake. But if you are clear about the type of image you want or the metaphor you are trying to illustrate, a few minutes searching through one of the major stock photography websites will often be fruitful. Stock images can cost as little as a $1 for a web-quality image and from $10 to several hundred for a print-quality image.

For an alternative to stock photography sites, try photo-sharing sites like Flickr.com where both professional and amateur photographers upload and share their photographs. Although it is often harder to find the right image on photo-sharing sites because the images typically aren't tagged and catalogued as thoroughly as they are on stock photography sites, you will usually find much more natural, "real life" photography. Photo-sharing sites will often be your best option if you need something gritty, funny, a little strange, or offbeat.

Regardless of where you find the image, you must always be aware of the copyrights attached to it, which determine what anyone other than the original creator can and cannot do with the image and under what terms. When you purchase photos from a stock photography site, you will be given options for the types of rights you want to purchase. On photo-sharing sites, you should look carefully to see what rights the photographer is offering.

One popular rights management program is Creative Commons, which allows creators of content, including photography, to specify the conditions under which others may use their photos at no cost. For example, under the Creative Commons "By" license, you can use a photo without paying the photographer as long as you give credit to that photographer wherever you use the photo. Other licenses limit the use of photos to noncommercial purposes and the extent to which a photo can be modified. Flickr allows you to search by the type of license you want.

Get in the habit of taking photos all the time (a great job for a volunteer), use stock photography or photo-sharing sites to fill in the gaps, and use photography in all of your communications offline and online.

SELECT THE BEST COMMUNICATIONS CHANNELS FOR YOUR COMMUNITY

You have your text and images. Now let's take a quick look at some of the most popular communications channels used by nonprofits today. Your marketing program will be most effective when you use multiple channels to get your message across and to promote conversations with your supporters. In many cases, you'll end up selecting the channel first, then developing the text and images for that channel. It doesn't matter so much which comes first, as long as the result accomplishes the goal of delivering your messages to your target communities.

Newsletter. The default communications channel to supporters for most non-profits is a newsletter, whether in print or email or both. Many nonprofits send quarterly newsletters, but if that's all you are sending, that's usually not enough to get your messages to stick. I believe it's better to produce a one- or two-page print newsletter or 500-word e-newsletter once a month than it is to produce an eight-page print newsletter once a quarter.

Other direct mail. From appeal letters and thank-you notes to event invitations and postcards, print mail (or snail mail) has always been central to nonprofit marketing. Many organizations are rightly reevaluating how much direct mail they send now and in what format because of cost considerations. Your organization needs to find the right mix of print and online communications, given your community, your messaging, and your own communications capabilities.

Website. Every nonprofit needs a basic website. Your website is your online home base; if you don't have one, your credibility immediately drops. Having a decent website is a sign of professionalism.

Social media. Social media, including sites like Facebook, LinkedIn, Instagram, YouTube, and Twitter, have changed forever how people connect and stay in touch. No matter your organization's mission, you should regularly use at least two of the major social networks. Choose the ones most popular with your target community or where your particular type of content works best.

Case studies, white papers, and reports. Publish your own reports and e-books as PDFs and offer them as free downloads on your website. You can sell them online, too.

Video and podcasts. It's easier and cheaper than ever to produce web-quality video and audio (podcasts). It's so much easier to share the human side of your work and the personality of your organization when people can hear your voice and see your face. Many people also prefer to get information by watching or listening rather than reading.

Photos and slide decks. Even if you don't have the audio to go along with them, photo essays and slide presentations can quickly convey information through the power of imagery, juxtaposed with a few words in the form of photo captions or slideshow text.

Advertising. Nonprofits are using print, TV, radio, and online advertising to promote their issues and organizations. Online advertising coupled with well-designed and inspiring landing pages can persuade people searching for information on various topics to become email newsletters subscribers and online donors.

Telephone calls. Although few people will admit to liking telemarketing, it can be effective when used in specific ways (for example, university students calling alumni, meeting reminders or urgent announcements sent by robocall to discrete, opt-in groups like club members).

Texting. The number of mobile phones worldwide has surpassed landlines, and some demographic groups on the other side of the digital divide, including some low-income populations, are connecting to the Internet primarily through mobile devices.

Events. Whether it's in-person or online, getting everyone together for a fun or educational event remains a tried-and-true method to reach your target communities. Events include workshops, webinars, parties, meet-ups, briefings, Internet radio shows, work camps, celebrations, and more.

Publicity. Getting media coverage of your organization and its work can bring your story to potential new supporters, whether it appears in print, online, on TV, or on the radio. Many practitioners now broaden this beyond mainstream media to include anyone creating content that could sway public opinion, such as bloggers or even individuals using Facebook or Twitter to spread messages to their friends.

Personal visits. Nothing beats the personal touch. Whether negotiating a case management plan for a client or a major gift, in-person meetings are best for convincing others to do something for us or with us.

Word-of-mouth. The younger you are, the more likely you are to trust what your friends say over any other way of receiving information. Even middle-aged people are jaded by advertising and overloaded by information. What we hear from people we trust matters, making word-of-mouth marketing extremely important to nonprofits (and it's cheap!).

USE MULTIPLE CHANNELS TO REINFORCE YOUR MESSAGE

Although some kind of newsletter is the default starting point for a nonprofit communications program, your newsletter shouldn't be your only means of communication. It's best to connect with your supporters through multiple channels. You can reinforce a message you sent via a postcard with an email. You can remind people about an event you marketed primarily through email by messaging the fans of your Facebook page or posting a reminder on your blog. Although you should publish an annual report at the end of your fiscal year, you should also be reporting on successes throughout the year in your newsletters and through social media. Reaching your supporters with the same message through multiple channels greatly increases the odds of them actually paying attention to it.

As much as possible, make your communications channels two-way, and let your community reply to you through multiple channels. Some will prefer to call you during office hours and others will prefer to send you an email or a message on Facebook in the evening. By using several communications channels, you give your supporters more options for communicating their opinions and ideas back to you.

One common concern about using multiple channels is the fear of repetition. But remember, repetition has its benefits in marketing. The conventional wisdom is that a person has to hear or see a message somewhere between three and seven times before it sinks in. But your supporters are not reading every single thing you send them. Even if they technically receive the same message in three different places, they may actually read or hear it in only one of those places, overlooking it in the other two. And people are not committing what they do read to memory, which means you need to deliver your message even more often – perhaps as many as 20 times before it really gets through.

At the same time, when people are connecting with you in multiple channels, you don't want to bore or annoy them with too much duplication. You can easily avoid that by simply remixing your content as part of a content creation strategy. While keeping your message consistent, you can use different words, visuals, formats, and channels to get that message across, so it feels fresh to your supporters but still reinforces a consistent message.

One downside of using multiple channels is that it makes it harder to measure the effectiveness of any one particular channel. Although you may be able to connect a certain level of fundraising income to a particular direct mail letter, for example, those donors may have been much more inclined to give because they received your email newsletter monthly throughout the year. Therefore, the newsletter is contributing to the success of the direct mail campaign. Difficulty in measuring the impact of your specific communications channels is a minor downside compared to the overwhelming benefits of reaching out to your supporters in multiple ways.

PUT YOUR MESSAGE WHERE YOUR COMMUNITY IS ALREADY GOING

One of the easiest ways to select the right channels is to think about where your target community is already going and to take your message to them there. Where do these people get their news? Do they read the paper, watch TV, listen to the radio, or spend most of their day online? Are particular groups of friends, family, or coworkers influential? Do they attend regular church services, or soccer practices, or Chamber of Commerce meetings? Where do they go during the day and at night? Where do they work, shop, and relax? What do they see, hear, taste, and touch throughout the course of the day? Are they on your mailing list now or not? These questions can help you figure out the right communications channel for your community and your message.

EXAMPLE: SELECTING CHANNELS TO REACH VOLUNTEERS

Let's take a look at which channels could work to get our four potential volunteers through the doors of our community center. Some channels will work for all of them and others will need to be tailored to the individual personas of Anna, Jessica, John, and Miguel.

First, we need to make sure that our website home page clearly and boldly says that we are looking for new volunteers. We discussed the kinds of messages we would use to describe the volunteer opportunities in Chapter 7, so we need to make sure that our website text and images reflect those specific messages. If we have a blog, we can ask some of our existing volunteers who are similar to our personas to blog about their volunteer experiences. We will also use our email newsletter and social media posts to spread the word to our existing supporters about the kind of volunteer opportunities available, again describing them in ways that will appeal to the four personas. The website, blog, email newsletter, and social media will all be clear that new volunteers should contact our volunteer coordinator, and we will provide their name, email address, and phone number everywhere we talk about volunteering.

Next, we'll want to drive traffic to our website by building up word-of-mouth marketing about volunteering with us. We'll think about where our personas are already going and try to get our messages out through those locations. We know that older community members like Anna hang out at the local coffee shop and the early yoga class at the gym, so we'll go talk to the people who work there and put up some flyers. Older people still watch network TV, so we'll work on getting some publicity with our local television station.

Jessica is the single mom who is trying to build her career skills. With this persona in mind, we'll talk to counselors at the local community college and job placement centers, making sure they understand how volunteering with us can build a résumé. We'll also leave some business cards or brochures with them. We might do the same with women's groups at local churches and business associations.

Our businessman, John, reads the paper and has lunch with the movers and shakers in town, so we'll use personal contacts we have on staff with the Chamber of Commerce, the newspaper editor, and other business leaders in our community, encouraging them to spread the word to their friends about ways they can give back.

To reach our college student, Miguel, we'll ask our existing college-age volunteers to set up social media posts and events to spread the word to their friends. We'll also talk to counselors and popular teachers at the local community college. Perhaps we can convince some instructors to offer course credit for volunteering.

IS PRINT PASSÉ?

The same people who believe that print marketing materials are passé are probably the ones who predicted the paperless office back in the early 1990s. Personal computing has dramatically *increased* paper use, not decreased it, as everyone can now write, design, and print whatever they want, at home and at work.

How we are communicating is changing, no question about it, and that means that the role of print is changing too. The print newsletter was once the mainstay of nonprofit communications, but the email newsletter has quickly taken its place. Although a print newsletter may or may not be a good approach, print is still an important channel for many organizations. Just like any other communications channel, it depends on who you are trying to reach and what messages you are sending.

If you are trying to reach people without computers or broadband access, or people who have email but rarely check it, then an email newsletter isn't really going to work well. Many fundraising studies support using multiple channels both offline and online to raise money, particularly from older generations (such as a direct mail appeal letter and email updates with success stories).

Don't do print just because you've always done it that way. But don't write off print as an outdated channel either.

CONVINCE YOUR SUPPORTERS TO OPEN YOUR EMAIL

Before your email newsletter and single-topic emails will be read, they have to be opened. Here are 10 tips for getting your nonprofit's email opened and read.

1. *Make the "From" field recognizable.* Provide consistency from issue to issue of your newsletter by using the same name/organization in the "From" field for each edition. Use a staff member's name if the majority of the people on the list will recognize it. Otherwise, use the organizational name or a combination of the two.

2. *Describe the candy, not the wrapper.* Use the subject line to tell us what goodies are inside this email, not about the packaging. In other words, don't put "Go Green Association Newsletter, Volume 5, Issue 7" in your subject line. Instead, tell us what's in this edition of the newsletter, such as "How to Live in Harmony with Backyard Wildlife."

3. *Change your subject line from edition to edition.* Some people will tell you that using the same subject line over and over works for them, but I believe that's probably the exception to the rule, as long as you are using a recognizable "From" field.

4. *Emphasize the personal value of your content.* It's the old "What's in it for me?" question. Why should I take precious time out of my busy day to read your email? I will, if you are providing information I want, need, or am curious about, or if reading your email will help me do something faster, cheaper, or easier or otherwise make my life more pleasant, enjoyable, or meaningful.

   Subject lines that make readers think "This is useful" or "This is timely" or "This is about me" will always work.

5. *Don't tell people what to do.* Although I always recommend that you include a call to action in every email (and with every email article),

some research shows that telling people what to do in the subject line itself can hurt your open rates. This is particularly true when asking people to help or donate or register. Specific calls to action are great within the body of the email, but for the subject line, lean toward the "personal value" words. For example, "Where to Dance All Night with Your Best Friends" will work better than "Register for Our All-Night Dance-a-thon Fundraiser." However, when there is a genuine sense of urgency, such as a disaster or a real deadline, including the call to action in the subject line is appropriate.

6. *Keep it short.* You'll find all kinds of advice on just how many characters are optimal for email subject lines. Some go as high as 60 characters, including spaces. Somewhere around 20 to 35 characters seems to be the ideal, but some people argue that even shorter is better. You can play with subject line length and see what works for you.

7. *Piggyback on hot topics and brand names.* Think about what's hot in the news right now. What products and services are people talking about now? How can you relate your work back to big brand names?

8. *Make it easy to read on mobile.* A simple one-column email is easiest to read on a small device. Be sure to review how your emails are appearing on smartphones or use any number of free services that will show you how they look on a variety of devices. Just search "preview email on multiple devices" for several options.

9. *Keep your mailing list clean.* Are you removing bouncing email addresses from your list or making sure that your email newsletter service provider does this for you? Continuously emailing bad addresses is one of the marks of a spammer, which can affect how many of your emails get delivered. Don't give the Internet service providers who trap spam for their customers a reason to block your email. We'll discuss email engagement in more detail in Chapter Thirteen.

10. *Send to your list regularly.* Your supporters will recognize email from you if you send it often. Try to send email at least once or twice a month at a minimum and adjust up from there as you have enough high-quality content.

CONCLUSION: FIND THE RIGHT MIX AND GIVE IT TIME TO WORK

The most creative, focused message won't motivate a single person if it's not delivered to your target community in a format they are likely to see. We are all inundated with information and messaging in all aspects of our lives. Even if the right message appears in the right place, if it only appears there once, it can be easily overlooked. Find the right mix of words, images, and communications tools to share your message with your target community, then stick with your marketing plan. Give it ample time to work. You'll tire of your nonprofit marketing program before your community will!

PART THREE

Building a Community of Supporters Around You

No matter what your mission statement says, all nonprofits share a common goal: to get certain people to think, feel, or act differently because you believe it will lead to some public good. You may want people to change their behavior or attitudes. You may want lawmakers or regulators to change policies. You may want your supporters to take certain actions or to donate their time or money. You may want to research, educate, or raise awareness about particular issues. These are big goals that will be hard to accomplish on your own.

But when you make nonprofit marketing a core part of your organizational management, you don't have to do it alone. Instead, you build a community of supporters around you. Nonprofit communications directors are turning into nonprofit community builders, organizers, and managers, as nonprofits recognize the value in letting their supporters connect with each other and the nonprofit's staff and volunteer leaders more regularly and more personally. As you build this community around you, you exponentially grow the number of people who are now helping you market your good cause.

In this section, you'll look at some of the basic steps in building your network of supporters: making it easy for people to find and to connect with your cause (Chapter 11), becoming an expert that the media and others turn to (Chapter 12), staying in touch and building engagement with your supporters through frequent communications (Chapter 13), and empowering your fans to build even more support for you (Chapter 14). Sounds good, doesn't it?

Make It Easy to Find You and to Connect with Your Cause

When Heidi Gollub started her job as chief marketing officer of Marathon Kids, which works to get kids moving, their blog had infrequent posts and no web traffic. That all changed with a Google Ad Grant and a renewed commitment to managing the blog's editorial calendar.

Heidi decided to start with some general content that PE teachers might like. "We published a blog post called 'Best Indoor PE Games' and created a Google Ad campaign targeting PE teachers," said Heidi. The post was read 46,904 times. She tried again, this time with "Best Outdoor PE Games" and that post was read 45,578 times. Heidi knew she was on to something!

From there, she created an editorial calendar around content geared toward making PE teachers' lives easier, while also positioning Marathon Kids as experts on PE curriculum and programming. She published two to four keyword-rich blog posts per month, including "PE Running Games," "23 Cool-Down Activities" and "Best Adaptive and Inclusive PE Games."

She also started listening more intently to her targeted community by joining Facebook Groups that elementary PE teachers use. Based on the questions she saw in those groups, she created additional content for her blog.

When she was ready to introduce a new program for teachers, Heidi used all of the popular blog posts to point readers to learn more about the program. "In the month that the program launched," said Heidi, "we had a record number of registrations, before the school year had even started in most states!"

Heidi made great management decisions. She decided who she wanted to reach. She listened to learn what content they needed. She delivered what they were seeking and drew the search traffic to her. Then she converted that search traffic and website visitors into program participants.

You might have different targeted communities, messages, and communications channels in mind, but you can make it just as easy as Heidi did for people to find you and to connect with your cause.

BE WHERE PEOPLE ARE SEARCHING FOR ORGANIZATIONS LIKE YOURS

Few people wake up and decide out of the blue to support a particular charity. It's much more likely that one of two scenarios will happen: the person will be referred to you by a trusted source, or the person will seek out an organization that can help her in some way, just as the PE teachers did with Marathon Kids.

In the first scenario, the person might hear about you from a friend who was talking over lunch about volunteering with your organization (we call that word-of-mouth marketing). Or your organization might be included in a story on the evening news program that this person watches every day (we call that publicity or earned media). Either way, this potential new supporter learns about your organization from a trusted source; what she hears piques her interest, and she seeks out additional informational about you.

In the second scenario, an event in a person's life, big or small, prompts her to seek answers to questions she has or motivates her to take some kind of action in her own life. Few people would think, "I want to find an animal rescue group and give them some money." Instead, they are much more likely to think, "I'm really tired of all the stray cats coming into our yard. We need to do something about this. I wonder who can help me?" Or "I'm ready to give in and get the kids a puppy. Where should I get one and what kind?" She connects with your mission or your programs and services before she connects with your organization itself, because it's your mission that meets some kind of need or touches on some values in her own life.

In both scenarios, you want this person to be able to easily find your organization, regardless of whether she heard about you from a trusted source or is trying to resolve a question or problem in her own life. Once she finds you, you want to offer ways to stay in touch with each other and to open the lines for two-way communication.

CREATE A VISIBLE AND ACCESSIBLE HOME BASE

Every nonprofit should have a primary home base. This is the place where you want people to start when contacting you for the first time. You'll put this on every publication you create. It's also the contact information that you want your current supporters to pass on to their friends. When they are having dinner together, and one friend mentions your organization to another, what do you want that person to write down on the cocktail napkin about how to contact you?

Your home base may be a physical location that you own or rent, where clients and supporters come regularly. In that case, you'll constantly promote your street address or easily identifiable location (for example, 1255 Main Street in Smithtown, or across the street from Smithtown Elementary School).

But many nonprofits don't have public offices or rarely have in-person visitors. Others use P.O. boxes, which people obviously can't visit. In these cases, promoting a physical address doesn't make much sense, because it doesn't allow that potential new supporter or client to find you quickly. Instead, you should emphasize a phone number, email address, website, or social media platform as your primary home base. For example, if you run a hotline, your toll-free phone number is a more appropriate home base to promote. If your staff are spread out across the country or work from home offices, using your website as your home base will make more sense. While possible, I don't recommend that you use social media as your primary home base, because you have far less control over what happens with your profiles long-term, especially compared to a website or even email.

When you have space, it's fine to include your complete contact information. But you'll often be required to include much less, and in these cases, go with that visible and accessible home base.

GIVE NEW CONTACTS MULTIPLE OPTIONS FOR STAYING IN TOUCH

Once a potential new supporter finds you through your home base, your website, social media, or some other venue, you need to offer at least one way for that person to connect with your organization so that you can stay in touch.

If they first found you online, they may provide you with only an email address. If they registered for an in-person event, you may have only a snail mail address, and that's fine. Many people will be reluctant to share all of their contact information with you until they trust that you won't abuse that information. Over time, try to develop a more complete contact profile for your supporters so you can contact them through multiple channels. It's extremely important that your contact with supporters be permission-based. In other words, they have indicated that they want to receive information from you and have given you permission to contact them.

KEEP YOUR WEBSITE IN GOOD SHAPE

The first friend that many of us turn to when we have questions these days isn't our college roommate, but Google or another search engine. You want to make sure that Google and other search engines produce *your* site as a top answer to the searcher's question. You do that in part by having a decent website that you update regularly and that others link to.

For most nonprofits, your website is the trunk of your online marketing tree. Everything you do online grows from and connects back to your website. Potential new supporters will also form their first impressions of you through your website, so make it a good one (the website and the first impression). I recommend the following 10-point checklist of questions to ask as you evaluate your current website or guide the creation of a new one.

1. Does the Domain Name Make Sense?

Use whole words if they are relatively short. Abbreviations can work too. For example, the Environmental Defense Fund can be found at edf.org. Environmentaldefense.org and environmentaldefensefund.org redirect automatically to edf.org. Note that their domain name is not some difficult-to-recall abbreviation like envdef.org. Those are the worst, because they are very difficult to guess and to remember. Shorter is better, because you'll leave less room for typos.

You should also consider purchasing multiple domain names as EDF has done. In real estate, it's location, location, location. Online, those locations are your domain names. I recommend that nonprofits buy not only the .org versions of their domain names, but also the .com and .net versions. When you don't buy all the versions, someone else will eventually snatch them up and most likely put up an advertising site. If the domains you want are not currently available, you can establish a monitoring account with your domain registrar, so you'll be notified if the current owners let their domain registrations lapse, making them publicly available again.

Also consider purchasing domain names that feature your keywords, project names, and so on. You can either forward these domains to a section of your main website or you can use them to create and market microsites, or mini websites that may or may not be part of your larger website. For example, the Humane Society of the United States owns StopPuppyMills.org and several other campaign-specific domain addresses that redirect to campaign pages on their website.

2. Do I Know Where I Am?

Can I tell after the briefest glance whose website I'm on? Are your logo and name right at the top? If your organization works only locally or regionally, it's also important that we quickly see exactly where you are. Include your city and state in a prominent location. This will help site visitors who may easily mistake you for a similar organization in a different area. For example, I live in Davidson County, North Carolina, but there is also a Davidson County, Tennessee, which includes Nashville. Nonprofits in areas with common place names should be very clear and up front on their home pages about which state they are in, especially when the place name is within the name of the organization.

3. Is There a Clear Path to Answers or Actions Visitors Are Most Likely Seeking?

To help focus your site on your visitors rather than on your organization itself, think about why people would come to your website in the first place. What three questions would they be seeking answers for? What three actions would they like to take (say, registering for an event, exploring your services, donating online)? The path to those answers and actions should be crystal clear on your home page. Within just a few seconds, can I see where I need to click to get those answers and take those actions?

Creating this kind of website requires that you understand your typical visitors well. Your website should reflect those people – the website visitors – more than it reflects the people who work at the nonprofit or the organization itself. You can achieve this by structuring the navigation of your website around the top answers they are seeking and actions they'd like to take.

For example, think about what people might want to do on a website for a Meals on Wheels chapter. They might want to sign up a loved one for meals.

They might want to volunteer to cook or deliver meals. Therefore, big buttons and menu navigation that say, "Get Meals" and "Deliver Meals" make a lot of sense.

4. Does the Home Page Include Images?

The web is a visual place, and every home page should include at least one image. Ideally, you will use your own photography, but if good photos aren't available, you can use high-quality stock photography too. Choose photos that make an impression on site visitors and give them additional information about your organization's work.

5. Can I Donate Online Easily from the Home Page?

Don't hide that "Donate Now" button where we have to search for it. Make it very easy to find and make it easy for supporters to fill out your online form by keeping the amount of required information to a minimum.

6. Are You Capturing Email Addresses?

Getting people to your website is the hard part. Now that you've got them there, don't let them just disappear back into cyberspace. The best way to turn a first-time website visitor into a long-term supporter is to start a conversation. To do that, you have to know who they are. Encourage visitors to stay in touch with you by signing up for an email newsletter, action alerts, or whatever you'd like to call your email correspondence. Make signing up for your email newsletter incredibly easy and obvious. Or offer a free download that requires registration. The point is to capture those email addresses so you can start a conversation with those website visitors.

7. Are People Featured?

Every nonprofit, even those focused on saving whales, needs to have pictures and stories featuring people on its website. Donors write checks to support the work of people trying to save the whales, not the whales themselves. Whale pictures are fine, but also feature your donors, volunteers, staff, partners, clients, and other people on your website doing the work they love on behalf of your cause.

8. Are There Stories on the Need or Successes?

Mission statements are usually tough to understand because they are written in jargon or nonprofit-ese that only insiders like staff and board members can understand. Yet that's often exactly what nonprofits post on their home pages, leaving your average website visitor confused about what it is you actually do.

In stark contrast, stories draw people in and really explain what it is you do. Stories are the easiest way to give examples of the need for your organization, the challenges you face, what you are doing to overcome them, and your successes. Tell short stories on your home page or link from your home page excerpts to the full story elsewhere on your website.

9. Is It Easy to Contact Staff?

Before a donor writes a big check, that person will probably want to talk to you. If someone is interested in partnering with your organization, that person will want to know which staff person to call to discuss a project. Don't make it hard to identify who's doing what. A full staff directory is ideal, but for larger organizations, including only executives, managers, and key contacts for the most common inquiries is fine.

10. Regularly Delete Out-of-Date Content

Outdated information on your website is the equivalent of mail and newspapers stacking up at the curb. Anybody in there? Everything OK? Let the world know that you are alive and well by keeping your website current. Otherwise they will assume that you've shut down.

IMPROVE YOUR SEARCH ENGINE RANKINGS

Enter virtually any term into a search engine like Google and you'll get back thousands, if not millions, of results. But what appears on the first page of results is most important. The overwhelming majority of people don't look past the first page of search results. That means you should try to optimize your website for the keywords that your targeted community is most likely using when searching.

Following the advice in the preceding checklist will help you improve your search engine rankings, because people are more likely to link to high-quality sites with up-to-date, interesting content. But there are also many small changes you can make, some editorial and some technical, that can also increase your search engine rankings. Hundreds of factors go into how websites rank, so it's impossible to review all of them. But here are few of the most important ones.

Offer a Responsive or Mobile Friendly Design

If your website doesn't look right on a phone, or if it loads too slowly, it won't rank as highly. Google and other search engines use a mobile-first index which means they review your site first based on what it looks like to a mobile user, followed by what it looks like on a desktop computer.

Decide on the Keywords for Each Page

Decide what each page on your website is about and use those keywords or phrases throughout that page, including in the page titles and throughout the page text. If you are linking out to another page on your site, make sure the linked (or anchor) text on the first page includes the keywords for the second page that you are linking to.

Add Keywords to Page URLs or Permalinks

If you have control over what appears in the actual URL for the page, put keywords there too. A URL like studies.htm tells the search engines very little, but one like early-child-education-impact-studies.htm says so much more.

Label Your Images

A photo called dogsreadyforadoption.jpg is more meaningful to search engines than image1234.jpg. Also, use the alt text to give the image a label, like "These dogs are now available for adoption." Not only will this help the search engines, but it's also required if you want your site to be useful to those with visual impairments.

SHOULD YOUR WEBSITE INCLUDE A BLOG?

I'm a big advocate of blogging for nonprofits because it's an easy, convenient way to create and share your articles and stories with supporters. Blogs can also help boost your search engine rankings. Keep in mind that you don't have to actually call it a blog. Many nonprofits use the blogging feature on their websites as more of a "news" or "resources" section.

To help you think through this question, here are my top five reasons why a nonprofit should have a blog and my top five reasons why a nonprofit shouldn't.

You *Do* Need a Blog If . . .

1. *You need to take people behind the scenes.* This is especially important for organizations that work in places people either can't get to easily on their own (for example, overseas or restricted areas like hospital wards or prisons) or are reluctant to visit, even if they could. For your supporters to really get what you do, they have to understand where you do it. Blogging lets you take them there by giving you a platform to share stories and photos over time, creating an ongoing narrative, post by post, all in one easily accessible place.

2. *You need a better way to organize the resources you have available.* If you see yourself as a service, training, or resource provider, you probably have a ton of information on your website that is actually pretty tough for people to find. One of the beautiful things about blogging is that categories and tags are a natural part of the software, so you can easily group items and your readers can easily find them.

3. *You need to react quickly.* If your organization responds to breaking news, I don't see how you can be effective online without a blog or a functional equivalent. You need a place to post your hot news.

4. *You need to incubate content for bigger publications.* If you produce reports, white papers, books, and the like, then a blog is perfect for your organization. It lets you publish bits and pieces as you create them and get comments from others who care about your issues. Then it's all right there when you are ready to create a larger publication.

5. *You need a better way to share the small stuff.* You have many wonderful little anecdotes that your supporters would love to hear. You also run across cool resources and surprising statistics all the time, but none of it really ranks as a post on its own, so you share the nuggets on social media. But compiling a lot of these related items into a round-up post is another great way to use a blog. That way the content isn't on social media alone.

You *Don't* Need a Blog If . . .

1. *Transparency is too scary.* Blogging is about sharing. If the idea of strangers getting a peek into your work makes you extremely nervous, then forget about blogging.

2. *Writing in a personal tone of voice is too hard.* Good blog writing is direct, conversational, and personal. If you are only comfortable writing as "the organization" rather than as a person working at the organization, then blogging may not be for you.

3. *Criticism is too scary.* If you only want to hear from people who agree with you, blogging is not for you. In my opinion, you can't turn off comments and still call what you are doing blogging. Yes, you need to moderate the incoming comments, but don't delete comments just because they are critical.

4. *You can't make the time.* Because of the chronological nature of blogging, people pay attention to how often you post. If you can't post at least once a week, blogging probably isn't for you.

5. *You can't articulate the value of your blog.* If you don't know how your blog fits into your nonprofit marketing strategy and what you want to accomplish with it, then don't do it.

GROW YOUR EMAIL LIST

Standard ways to build an email list include putting the sign-up box in your website template so it appears on every page of your site and requesting email addresses on every form you ask people to complete. But you can grow your list much more quickly if you also use the following approaches:

- *Entice readers with promised benefits – and deliver.* Email addresses are valuable. What are you giving your supporter in exchange for that valuable email address? Don't just say, "We want to send you a newsletter." Explain what kind of interesting, exclusive, and timely information your supporters will receive from you in that newsletter.

- *Use a website pop-up or lightbox.* Love them or hate them, they work. Invite people to join your community. Offer something special. Make a promise to keep them updated on the news they care about.

- *Offer a special download.* If many people approach your organization with the same kinds of questions, create a guide or white paper with the answers. Explain clearly that when they register for the free download, they'll also be added to your e-newsletter list.

- *Try a quiz.* Some quizzes are goofy personality testers, but others are quite serious. Using an online quiz provider, you can make opting into your email list either required or recommended to get the quiz results.

- *Collect email addresses offline.* Don't get stuck in the single-channel mindset. When you see supporters in person, ask for their email addresses. Bring a paper sign-up sheet to your events and leave one on your reception desk. Fill in the gaps by calling supporters and asking for permission to email them.

- *Make changing an email address easy.* Ideally, subscribers to your newsletter should be able to update their own email addresses with just a few clicks. The harder you make it (for example, forcing them to unsubscribe and resubscribe), the more likely they are to drop off your list for good.

- *Put their privacy concerns to rest.* Many people assume that when they give their email address to a nonprofit, the organization will sell or rent it to other causes, creating an unwanted flood of spam. Put your supporters at ease by assuring them that you will not rent, sell, or otherwise share their email addresses with others (and then don't!).

No matter which tactics you use to build your list, you should always make it clear that unsubscribing will be painless and that you will not sell subscriber addresses to anyone else. That's the best way to establish the trust you'll need to succeed with your email marketing campaigns.

BUILD YOUR SOCIAL MEDIA PRESENCE

Social media has revolutionized the way people not only use the Internet but also connect with other human beings across the street and around the planet. No one can say for sure how long the services popular when this book was published – like Facebook, Twitter, and YouTube – will be around, but the concept of social media – allowing people not only to create content, but to share it, talk about it, and remix it – is here to stay. I recommend that you commit to providing good, consistent content on two social media networks and set up minimal accounts on others.

Which ones you prioritize will depend on the type of content that you can easily create and who the typical users of those sites are. Some are more dominated by visuals than others. Some are better for breaking news and others excel at conversation.

The best ways to build your list of followers vary somewhat from social network to social network. But no matter which sites you prefer, I recommend that you be personal and practical.

Be personal by sharing the journey of your organization in an authentic, behind-the-scenes way, especially on any of the various Stories sections. Have a service mentality where you connect one-on-one with people. Show up and hang out by using livestreaming, events, or exclusive areas like Facebook Groups.

Be practical by knowing your content niche and focusing on those topics. Pay attention to what is working and what's not and continue to evolve your content as you learn what's most relevant to your followers. Repurpose that content so that you can create less but share more.

CONCLUSION: DON'T LET POTENTIAL SUPPORTERS SLIP AWAY

Nonprofit communicators spend a great deal of time creating content to attract website visitors, and yet a very small percentage – low single digits – of people who visit most nonprofit websites provide their email address to the organization by registering for email updates or taking some other action online. To move beyond merely being found by a potential supporter online, you have to provide multiple opportunities for people to connect and converse with you. Be visible, and when those people find you, don't let them slip away. Offer them an easy, meaningful way to take the next step.

Become an Expert Source for the Media and Decision Makers

For 35 years, American Rivers has released an annual report called *America's Most Endangered Rivers*®, spotlighting 10 rivers that need urgent public action to protect their health. Journalists, decision makers, and other conservation organizations anticipate the report's release every April.

Amy Souers Kober, vice president for communications at American Rivers, was all ready to release the 2020 report. Then the COVID-19 pandemic hit.

"As the coronavirus coverage saturated the news, we struggled to see how a river story could break through," said Amy. Plus, as the economy nose-dived, news organizations lost ad revenue and many journalists were furloughed. Some partners asked them to delay or cancel the release of the 2020 report.

"We considered our options, including postponing the release. But the question remained: postpone until when? One thing we had on our side was the theme of the 2020 report: flooding and climate change. The top three rivers on the list – the upper Mississippi, lower Missouri and Big Sunflower – are all threatened by outdated approaches to managing floods," said Amy.

Amy's team quickly adapted the call to action. In addition to asking decision makers to improve watershed management and give rivers room to flood safely as planned, they also asked officials to ensure that if a flood happened, people would be safe from the coronavirus too, whether they were stacking sandbags in a crowd of neighbors or taking refuge at a packed emergency shelter. They also talked about the imperative for people to have clean water for personal hygiene during the pandemic. "We used our platform to spotlight the colliding disasters of coronavirus and flooding, and we put public pressure on decision makers to act immediately," said Amy.

In addition to updating the messaging, American Rivers also had to adjust its strategy. In a typical year, they would go big on report release day, generating hundreds of news hits in 24 hours. "Instead, we decided not to rely solely on release day coverage. We'd look for opportunities to tell the story in the media, on social media, and with decision makers in the weeks and months to come. We knew we had to embrace creativity and flexibility," said Amy. Her team doubled down on digital, creating more video content and a much more extensive social media toolkit for partners than ever before.

"We expected a relatively quiet release on April 14, but we were wrong. It was one of our most successful Endangered Rivers releases ever. We got more media hits than the previous year, including high-profile stories in *USA Today* and the *Chicago Tribune*. Associated Press stories ran in the *New York Times*, *Washington Post*, and scores of local and regional outlets nationwide," said Amy.

As Amy's story makes clear, if you understand what's newsworthy and you give reporters what they need, getting news coverage is possible, even when it feels on the surface like maybe your stories aren't that compelling or timely.

In this chapter, let's look at several ways to get more media coverage and to position your organization as an expert source.

WHY SOME GROUPS GET THE CALL AND OTHERS DON'T

Why, your board president asks, isn't your organization in the news? After all, media coverage is one important way for potential new clients, participants, supporters, partners, and donors to learn about your organization. When you appear in respected publications produced by others, some of that respect rubs off on you in the readers' or viewers' eyes (assuming the mention was positive, of course).

Some people would answer the board president's question defensively and blame the reporters for not doing a thorough job researching who's really doing what in the community. Others might respond with jealousy and try to discredit the contributions of the other groups who are getting all the attention. Still others would shrug, completely mystified by how these organizations manage to get so much attention from the news media.

The groups that get the call are perceived as *expert sources*. Nonprofits that are viewed as experts by the media, decision makers, and their professional colleagues may reach the top of the call list through some intangibles like finesse, luck, and personality. But they get there primarily through hard work.

Being viewed as an expert source is a great nonprofit marketing strategy because it can produce lots of publicity. Other people, nonprofits, and media outlets – often with greater influence and reach than your organization – write and talk about you. Unlike advertising or marketing communications that you create and distribute yourself, this is publicity you don't have to pay for!

The nonprofit sector as a whole is well positioned to be considered a source of expertise by the media, policymakers, and the public for several reasons. First, a certain level of purity is associated with the nonprofit sector. You're supposed to be nonpartisan. You're supposed to have a social or civic-minded purpose. Nearly all nonprofits have a mission that is easily tied to a public benefit rather than to personal glory or money. That altruism makes you trustworthy.

The nonprofit sector as a whole is generally not considered to be very powerful. In polls, Americans say they would actually like to see nonprofits have more power and more decision-making authority in our society. Power is often seen as a corrupting influence, and because people consider nonprofits to be one of the less powerful sectors of society, being a nonprofit increases your credibility.

Also, you are doing interesting work. You're helping real people with real problems. Nonprofits have great anecdotes and access to people with amazing personal stories related to all of the hot issues of the day. The media loves a good story, and nonprofits have both stories to tell and access to plenty of people to interview.

But being a nonprofit alone won't position you as an expert source. You can't wait on the sidelines assuming people will call you. You have to get up off the bench and into the game, first by understanding the five qualities of a good expert source and then by pursuing seven strategies that raise your visibility as an expert.

THE FIVE QUALITIES OF A GOOD EXPERT SOURCE

To be a good expert source, you have to embody five qualities. You need to be accessible, cooperative, and trustworthy, and you need a well-understood niche and solid track record.

Be Accessible

The first and most important quality of an expert source for the news media is being accessible. A reporter or an editor on deadline will always pick the person she can reach quickly over the smartest person who's nearly impossible to get ahold of, especially on nights and weekends. You may be the best source on paper – you may have the best quotes and the best information – but if journalists can't reach you when the deadline clock is ticking down, they will run that story without you.

Make getting in touch with you easy by publishing several different ways to contact you, including off-hours phone numbers, on your website. If you are serious about wanting more press coverage, then you need to make your cell phone number publicly available. If you aren't comfortable listing these numbers online, then include them in your voice mail greeting on your office line.

The same goes for your email address. Some organizations try to mask email addresses from website spammers by using web contact forms instead. But reporters don't want to use a web form; they want to reach you, the expert, directly. Rather than hiding your email address from people whom you really do want to hear from, set up a good spam filter instead.

Be prepared to take phone calls in the evenings and on weekends. Media deadlines are often outside the typical 9:00 a.m. to 5:00 p.m., Monday through Friday schedule. That doesn't mean you have to take a reporter's call immediately and spend a half-hour answering questions during family dinner time. But it does mean that you should return voice mails promptly. If you do answer the call, it's fine to ask whether the reporter is on deadline and to schedule a better time to talk, whether it's in 30 minutes or the next day.

Be Cooperative

When someone calls a person they expect to be an expert, they are looking for the "Bingo!" moment. That's when you give them something they are looking for, perhaps an interesting story, a surprising statistic, and an intriguing quote. Whatever it is, in their own minds, as you are speaking, they think, "Bingo! That's just what I needed! I called the right person!"

You get to the "Bingo!" moment by listening. Let your callers set the agenda. They are calling you because they have specific questions, or they have a particular angle that they're working. Even if you think the caller is asking a really dumb or irrelevant question, answer it. If you don't answer their questions first, you will be seen as uncooperative and likely won't be called again.

Focus on what they're interested in, at least at first. Once you've answered those initial questions, you can start to steer the conversation in another direction. You might say, "Did you know . . . ?" or "Have you thought about . . . ?" You can lead the caller down another path that you think is more interesting or newsworthy.

Reporters in particular also love brief, but substantive answers. Although it can be difficult to do without practice, try to talk in bullet points or sound bites. Part of being an expert is anticipating the kinds of questions people have about your topic, and knowing your talking points so well that they smoothly roll off your tongue, no matter how much you may be caught off guard when the call comes in. Give reporters those nuggets of information and those short quotable quotes, in plain language. You won't find jargon in the newspaper or on TV, so don't use it in an interview with a reporter. The only exception would be with writers for trade press magazines who are familiar with your lingo. They can use it because their readers know it and use it too.

Being cooperative also means being resourceful for whoever is calling on you as the expert. Offer other sources of information. Give them other experts' names and phone numbers and email addresses. Be as helpful as you can in identifying people for the "person on the street" perspective. Turn them onto really good websites where they can find some good background information or statistics for the story.

Own a Well-Understood Niche

You don't know everything. No one does. So, don't pretend that you do. Instead, narrow down the areas that you want to be known for. What is your little piece of the larger pie of expertise in your field? How is your particular perspective different from those of other experts?

Let's say you work in animal rights, and a reporter is working on a story about how animals are treated in circuses and water parks. That reporter will want to talk to somebody who knows about wild animals in captivity. They will not be interested in talking to an animal rights advocate who spends most of her time on issues that affect cats and dogs.

In this case, putting yourself out there as an advocate for animals is not going to be enough to put you on that reporter's call list, even if she does know who you are. Your area of expertise is too broad. Instead, you need to narrow it down and put yourself out there as an expert on specific issues, such as how dolphins behave in entertainment venues.

Once you narrow down your niche, you want other experts in your larger field to recognize your expertise so that they can refer misdirected calls they receive to you. In our example, you might professionally befriend animal experts who deal with factory farming issues. If you get calls about pigs and cows, you can pass on their contact information. If they get calls about water parks, they can refer them to you. Hone in on what you are good at, what you know a lot about, and where you have bountiful resources to fall back on if you can't answer the caller's questions.

Build a Solid Track Record

The more often you are quoted, the more likely others will call you. But even without a solid track record, you can still establish some credibility, starting with your job title. Executive directors are more likely to be quoted than executive assistants. If you don't have a decent title, play up your experience instead. Create a short tagline for yourself that quickly explains why you would make a great source:

- Twenty years of experience living and working with homeless people
- Raised $5 million to provide low-income children with health care
- Managed a spay-neuter program that treated 700 cats and dogs in one summer

In addition to being cooperative, being consistent will also add to your track record. You want to be known for talking intelligently about your issues. You want to be known for returning phone calls and emails promptly. You want to be known for giving the good quotes. You want to be known for a wide-ranging network of people and giving good referrals. Even when you don't know the answers yourself, you can build your track record as a great expert source simply by knowing where else to go for the information.

Be Trustworthy

The fifth quality of a great expert source is being trustworthy. According to 2020 Gallup poll, nurses, engineers, medical doctors, pharmacists, dentists, and police officers are the most trusted professions. Conversely, some of the least trusted are members of Congress, insurance and car salespeople, and stockbrokers.

What's the difference? The most trusted group of professionals helps people, saves lives, and values training and objectivity. They don't have a particular vested interest, and they tend to stay out of the fray. The least trusted group, on the other hand, is often considered disingenuous, shallow, and greedy.

Nonprofits are generally trusted more than other institutions, including organized religion, banks, businesses, the media, and government, according to a 2018 report from the Better Business Bureau's Wise Giving Alliance.

So how can your nonprofit be a strong advocate for your cause, be politically powerful, and still remain trustworthy in the eyes of the public? It's all about transparency. You are what you are, and you should be completely honest and confident about it. There's no pretense in your communications and no hidden agendas in your marketing. You remain true to your public mission as a nonprofit and recognize opposing views with respect.

SEVEN STRATEGIES TO RAISE YOUR PROFILE AS AN EXPERT SOURCE

Now that you understand what people are looking for in an expert source and you are working to embody these five qualities, how do you go about raising your visibility so people know you exist and how to reach you? Work through the following seven strategies.

Pass the Background Check

People want to check you out before they call you. This is true for reporters, publishers, conference organizers, and anyone else who is thinking about asking for your expertise. Google is the background checker of choice when people are looking for expert sources, which means you need a good website.

On your website, you should have a basic online press kit. Include a short, simple explanation of what your organization does, for whom, and why. Include some good stories that demonstrate both the need for your organization and your successes. Add links to other articles, both those that have quoted you and those you have written yourself. You might also include statistics relevant to your cause and frequently asked questions (FAQ).

Include short bios for key staff members, with photos, that include both professional credentials and some personal details as well, so we see them as real human beings. Add contact information next to each name.

Work the Word of Mouth

Testimonials from others about how helpful, insightful, and smart the people in your organization are will go a long way in generating more calls for your expertise. Gather these short quotes from surveys, comment forms, your email box, and anywhere else you find people saying nice things about you and your work. It's best to use the person's name, so ask permission to include the testimonial on your website. If obtaining permission is impractical or impossible (for example, taking comments from anonymous evaluation forms where you spoke at a conference), simply list the person's relationship to you (for example, annual conference attendee).

Just as you want others to be generous with their praise of and referrals to you, you need to be equally generous in talking about the good works and expertise of others. Remember, you are focusing on one particular piece of the pie as your expertise. Be friendly with people claiming those other pieces of pie that are not as important to you. Lavish praise on them, and they'll notice you and remember you the next time someone calls them looking for your kind of expertise.

Nurture Big Brains and Big Mouths

If your organization's staff includes grand thinkers and great talkers, capitalize on that. Get out there and let people know what you're thinking and share those opinions. Big ideas and big opinions get people excited and generate headlines. Nonprofits with organizational personalities that are like the wallflower at the school dance will have a harder time being recognized as an expert than groups that are the life of the party.

If you don't have those big brains and big mouths on staff, then create some partnerships with others who do. Seek out academics, independent consultants, or authors who believe in your cause and your work but are better spokespeople than your staff members. Give them a title, even if the position is unpaid. Your organization becomes, in effect, their public voice and they become your expert source for the media. You work together to raise both of your profiles.

Publish Constantly

Most highly visible experts are publishing constantly. Although books are still great credibility boosters, they are very time-consuming to produce. To more quickly raise your visibility and improve your search engine rankings at the same time, publish online instead. Online publishing through websites, blogs, email newsletters, and podcasts is both fast and affordable.

Write an e-book or white paper that people can download for free from your website. Publish case studies, Q&A interviews, and how-to articles on your website. Blog about your work, providing a behind-the-scenes perspective. Write articles for association newsletters. Record yourself speaking about a topic and offer it as a podcast.

But don't publish about just anything. Remember, you want to build your reputation within your particular niche. Be strategic about how much you publish on various topics.

Listen for Opportunities to Speak Up

You can also participate in services created especially to connect expert sources and journalists. Help a Reporter Out (HARO) and Profnet compile requests for sources from journalists and connect them with experts.

When using services like these, it is essential that you respond only when your expertise matches well what the journalist is requesting. Off-topic and "I just wanted to introduce myself" responses to the specific inquiries posted through these services are not appreciated.

Answer Questions

Of course, journalists aren't the only ones seeking experts. Other professionals and the public are doing the same thing for their own needs. This is especially true on social media. Sites like LinkedIn, Facebook Groups, Reddit, and Quora are full of people with questions looking for answers from trusted sources like you.

You can also answer questions on your own website by setting up a FAQ page where visitors can submit questions or by holding online office hours in which you use a chat or instant messaging service to communicate with visitors in real time.

Teach Courses

Look into opportunities to share your expertise specifically with people who are seeking education on your topics. You can pursue formal teaching opportunities at local colleges and universities, including professional certificate programs. You can teach through associations, especially those that offer certifications that require continuing education credits. You can also set up your own workshops or webinars to share what you know and teach others how to complete those tasks at which you excel.

HOW TO PITCH YOUR STORY TO THE MEDIA

If you've never called a reporter to pitch a story before, relax. It's not that hard, if you follow these tips.

Skip the "blanket pitch." Don't contact every single reporter you can think of with the same pitch. It doesn't work. You have to personalize for each reporter.

Know your "newsy" hook. Is your story timely or unusual? Will it impact many people, or does it involve a prominent person? Does it have a compelling human-interest angle? Study the kinds of articles and broadcasts produced by the media outlets you are calling to get a sense for what they consider newsy.

Know your angle with each particular reporter. Sometimes you end up calling a general assignment reporter, and that's fine. You can go with a more straightforward pitch. But if you want your story in the business section, you need to pitch a business reporter, and your story should have a clear business angle. Nonprofit events could appear in virtually every section of the paper with the right angle and press release content (include quotes from elected officials if you are trying for the "Local" section or talking to the government beat reporter, quotes from business leaders if you are trying for the business section, and so on).

Connect your pitch to past reporting if you can. If the reporter has previously written about your topic or organization, definitely mention that (for example: "You wrote a great story about this in May, and I think this would be an excellent follow-up . . .").

Offer more than a press release. Will there be good photo opportunities? Can you put the reporter in touch with several people to interview? Any behind-the-scenes tours of particularly interesting or exclusive venues or backstage interviews with big keynote speakers or high-profile guests?

Practice your pitch. Practice getting your pitch down to 30 seconds, with the most important information in your first sentence. Most reporters will have no problem interrupting you and telling you they aren't interested if you don't grab them fast. You'll hear something like "It's not right for us," "Timing isn't good," a flat-out "No thanks," or "I don't know; I'll call you back" – which usually means no.

Don't get defensive or abusive if the reporter says no. Don't insult the reporter by saying things like, "Wow, you really don't get it" or "You are really missing out on the biggest story of the year." Reporters know better than you what they cover; if it really is the biggest story of the year, and the reporter turns it down, it's because your pitch is no good.

Here's a sample pitch.

Reporter

John Smith:	Hello, John Smith.
You:	Hi, John. My name is Bob Evans with Save the Squirrels. I have a story for you. [Note, you aren't saying, "I have the best story ever" or "a story you'd be an idiot to pass up" — keep it as a straightforward suggestion.]

or

You:	Hi, John. My name is Bob Evans with Save the Squirrels. I'd like to pitch a story to you really quickly if you have a minute. [Yes, it's OK to call what you are doing pitching. That's the term for it. The reporters know that's what you are doing, so it's no big deal to say it.]
Reporter:	You've caught me at a bad time; I'm right in the middle of something . . . [But he doesn't blow you off entirely.]
You:	I'll make it really quick, I promise . . .

or

Reporter:	OK, go ahead.
You:	[Launch right into it! No need for small talk or a bunch of background; just get to the point.] Our local squirrel population has been decimated, and on Saturday we are holding a special Dog Walk and Festival at City Park to raise money for a breeding program. Dogs love to chase squirrels, and dog owners all over town are reporting high levels of depression since the dogs have nothing to chase now. We are expecting at least a hundred people and dogs at the festival, and we'll have all kinds of fun contests, including a Dog/Owner Look-Alike Contest and an *American Idol*–style howling contest where the fire department will sound the truck sirens to get the dogs going. It's going to be lots of fun, with great photo opps, and all of the money will go directly to solving our local squirrel problem.

Reporter:	Do you have any numbers on the problem?
You:	Yes, a university study showed that our squirrel population is down by 50 percent.
Reporter:	How do we know the dogs are depressed?
You:	Dog owners can tell, and vets across town are being asked for antidepressants.
Reporter:	Any vets actually giving out the pills?
You:	Yeah, I can put you in touch with one or two. Do you want me to email you the press release for the festival and some vet contacts?
Reporter:	Sure. I'll see what I can do.
You:	Thanks, John. Let me give you my cell phone number . . .

It's really that simple. But notice how the reporter went off on a tangent with the dog depression rather than focusing on the Dog Walk and Festival? This happens all the time! Keep in mind that reporters decide what the story really is. You can always try to steer them back to your angle, but ultimately the reporters will decide what to write about or whether to cover it at all.

Respect that, and don't get pushy or critical about their decisions. A story about vets prescribing antidepressants that mentions your festival is better than no story at all! And now you know the reporter a little better and can come back next time with an even more focused pitch for John Smith.

Reporters tend to be skeptical by nature, so don't be put off if one quizzes you or doesn't seem particularly excited. Work your pitch and follow up with whatever the reporter asks for. Remember, you need each other. Reporters need good stories, and you need the publicity. Build those relationships, give reporters what they need (good stories!), and you'll get some great press in return.

BE READY TO NEWSJACK

David Meerman Scott coined the term "newsjacking" in 2011. He defines it as the art and science of injecting your ideas into a breaking news story, so you and your ideas get noticed.

In their book, *Modern Media Relations for Nonprofits: Creating an Effective PR Strategy for Today's World*, Peter Panepento and Antionette Kerr offer six tips for successful newsjacking.[1]

1. **Prepare your key messages in advance**. Before you begin scouring Twitter or your local newspaper for newsjacking opportunities, you have to first know what you want to talk about when opportunities arise. Take time to have a clear sense of your larger communications goals and the key messages you want to express. This will help ensure that you're saying the right things if a reporter does show up with a microphone or notebook in hand.

2. **Develop relationships.** To newsjack effectively, it helps to know how to get to the right reporter or editor quickly. Sending pitches to general email boxes or calling a main newsroom line isn't likely to get you results. Instead, identify some outlets that are of high value to your organization, pay attention to who is getting bylines around the topics you care about, and start to build relationships with them.

3. **Create protocols.** News moves quickly, and newsjacking requires an ability to make your pitch while a story is still hot. As a result, it's important to prepare your organization to make fast decisions. If you have to go through multiple layers of approval before you can send a news release or call a reporter, you're likely to lose opportunities.

4. **Pay attention.** To jack the news, you have to know the news. This means following key news outlets regularly – as well as paying attention to social media – to see what news is breaking.

5. **Act quickly.** Newsjacking is most effective when you make your pitch shortly after the news first breaks, and before the "second day" reports come out offering context. It's a great goal to be in the second paragraph of a second-day news story.

6. **Speak sensitively.** Newsjacking can backfire if you don't employ it with tact and sensitivity. The Internet is littered with examples of companies and nonprofits that have tried to attach themselves to tragedies or disasters and have come across as tone-deaf or opportunistic. Make sure you're acting tastefully and that your effort to draw attention is something that you and your organization will be proud of later.

Following Antionette's advice, Tom Harrison, the director of the North Carolina Black Bear Festival and Bear-ology Museum in Plymouth, North Carolina, was able to turn a sad story into a newsjacking and advocacy success.[2]

In 1972, two bears were killed on North Carolina highways. By 2017, that number was over 200. Tom wanted to warn drivers and share safety advice on behalf of the museum and festival to save bears' lives.

After working with Antionette, Tom asked local law enforcement to give him a call the next time a car collided with a black bear in his area. When that happened, Tom quickly made his way to the scene, where he took photos of both the mangled car and the dead bear.

Bear collisions were on the rise, but not trending in the media before Tom's photo of the dead bear went viral with over 400,000 views in 24 hours and a total of 3,003 shares.

This might seem like a morbid story, but sometimes startling visuals are what it takes to grab people's attention. Tom knew that posting a photo of the dead bear was risky – but real. Tom also gave other photo options, such as the mangled car. Ultimately, the photo of the bear is the one that went viral on Facebook.

This tragedy resonated with those who love the bears and drivers alike. It provided an opportunity for people to learn about driving safely during bear mating season. In the end, Tom didn't get a lot of pushback about the photo, but inevitably, when you are talking about a hot topic, someone will be bothered. Antionette encourages you to tread lightly and to check in with your leadership to discuss the appropriate messaging and potential risks and rewards before posting.

Tom was also ready to give a good interview. He spent time studying the rising black bear collision crisis and was ready to offer statistics, other experts, and tips for drivers when tragedy struck.

As a result of Tom's preparation and ability to newsjack the story, the Black Bear Festival received coverage from across the state and country. Overnight, Tom was identified as a thought leader and expert. More than a dozen media outlets contacted Tom for interviews and photo permissions, many of whom said they had never heard of the festival or the museum before.

WHO IS THE EXPERT? YOU OR THE ORGANIZATION?

Before you launch a publicity campaign using these strategies to raise your visibility as an expert, it's important to distinguish between marketing your nonprofit as the expert and marketing individual staff members as experts.

Although you can do both, you should be clear about your intentions from the start.

Many times, it will make sense for a nonprofit to identify just one or two people as their primary spokespeople, and this is often determined by job description. Even if you are promoting the organization as the expert, it's only natural that some people will associate that expertise with the person instead. If one of those people moves on to another job, they may or may not take some of the credibility with them.

Be upfront in your staff discussions about marketing your experts, and you can avoid any uncomfortable feelings later about personal agendas and career advancement.

CONCLUSION: CREATE SOMETHING NEW AND SHARE IT

You can't become the kind of expert that others want to quote without doing the hard work to create that expertise. For many organizations, this means performing original research or analyzing data generated by others in innovative ways. That means you are building time into the life of your nonprofit to do your homework, to think about issues and approaches, and to share what you have learned. Hoarding information and ideas and then expecting others to clamor around your feet for words of wisdom simply doesn't work anymore; there are too many other experts – self-described or otherwise – right around the corner or a simple Google search away who are willing to give away what they know for free.

Find your niche. Work hard to create something new. Have something interesting to say. Then share it with others. That's how you become known as an expert source.

Build Engagement: Stay in Touch and Keep the Conversation Going

When Neely Conway started her job as the email engagement director for a large national nonprofit, she saw that the organization was creating great content and had a strong website, but email engagement was low. After investigating the organization's email metrics, she concluded that they had an email deliverability problem. In other words, although they were sending out timely and relevant emails, too many of those messages weren't landing in inboxes (many were going to spam).

The nonprofit was trapped in a vicious cycle: fewer people were opening emails and clicking on links, so the email inbox providers (the Googles and Microsofts of the world) started sending more of their emails to the spam folder. As more email goes to spam, even fewer people see them, so engagement falls even further, and so on.

Neely knew how to break the cycle. "We growth-hacked our deliverability," she said, "by focusing on list hygiene, segmenting and personalizing our message, and deploying automated re-engagement campaigns."

She started by removing the people who hadn't opened an email in the last 90 days from their regular communications. "Our goal was to focus on those subscribers who wanted to hear from us," said Neely. "But we didn't let go of the others right away. We developed a three-part re-engagement email series that centered the content we thought would resonate. We ensured they had an opportunity to follow us on social media, to participate in online learning campaigns, and to bookmark our website."

Next, Neely focused on communicating with the people who were engaged, or those opening at least one email in the last 90 days. "We asked people to reply to or forward our emails, a deliverability hack that has proven effective," said Neely. Inbox providers look for replies and forwards as one measure of email engagement. "We began including messaging in our email welcome series and re-engagement campaigns, asking people to reply with any questions. This approach offered a personal touch while also gathering feedback from our subscribers," she said.

Finally, the most important and effective tactic was to segment and personalize the messages they sent. "Email marketing is most effective when communications feel high-touch and customized to the individual subscriber," said Neely. Instead of sending everything to everyone, they began segmenting their mailing list based on user behavior (e.g. who was interested in what based on their online activity). "We wanted our email communications to look like they were sent to one individual when in reality, they were sent to 60,000," she said.

These tactics worked. By cleaning up their mailing list, segmenting and personalizing their messages, and using automated re-engagement campaigns, they not only improved their email deliverability (messages going to the inbox rather than spam), but their overall email engagement as a whole. "In under six months, we were able to increase our email engagement by 17 percent. Additionally, our website form conversion rates have more than doubled," said Neely. "This is just the beginning for us. Now that we're landing in the inbox to a highly engaged community, we've built a solid foundation. And now, we get to focus on building these relationships in an even more meaningful way."

Neely's story demonstrates the challenges that nonprofits face with staying in touch and keeping the conversation going – and her story was limited to email engagement.

Once you've connected with a potential supporter and you have at least one way to stay in touch, you need to start a conversation with that person. Only by keeping the lines of communication open in both directions will you turn that initial interest in your cause into a long-term commitment to it. In fact, this is absolutely essential if you eventually plan to ask this new supporter for money. As Penelope Burk says in *Donor-Centered Fundraising*, "Meaningful information on their gifts at work is the key to donors' repeat and increased giving. Communication is the process by which information is delivered. Fundraising underperformance, therefore, is actually a failure to communicate."[1]

Your job now, regardless of whether you consider new contacts to be fundraising prospects or not, is to educate, to pique their interest in what's possible, and to inspire them to help you achieve your mission. To build that kind of relationship over time, you need to communicate regularly. On a very practical level, you need to consider the kind of information that your new and current supporters want to receive from you and how often and in what formats they prefer to receive it. Likewise, you need to consider your capacity to meet those expectations.

IS YOUR CONTENT LIKE A GOOD GIFT OR A BAD GIFT?

Let's have a little fun and apply what we've learned about creating personas to nonprofits as content publishers. When I think of the types of nonprofit newsletter content I see in particular, it reminds me of being a kid anticipating presents from family. Think back to a time of year when you knew everyone in your family would give you presents, whether it was your birthday, Christmas, or some other special celebration. Whose gifts did you want to tear open right away, and whose were sure to disappoint?

Odds are the good gift givers were the people who listened well and cared about what you wanted. They paid attention and were thoughtful in making gift choices, focusing on what your reaction to the present would be.

What about the gift givers who weren't so great? It might have seemed like giving you a present was more like a chore, a duty, or a hassle to them. They probably didn't put much thought into it, and certainly didn't ask you want you wanted. They fulfilled their obligations based on what they wanted, not on what you wanted.

Let's create some personas to demonstrate how this works. Remember, personas are by nature a form of stereotyping. If you don't recognize these types of family gift givers in your own life, you may recognize them from any number of bad holiday movies.

But the real question is will you recognize your organization's approach to communications in these gifting styles?

Curmudgeonly Uncle

He thinks kids have it so easy these days – they're all spoiled brats who have no idea what the real world is like. To be honest, he doesn't really care what you want for your birthday, because you probably don't deserve anything anyway.

Curmudgeonly Uncle nonprofits are bitter that they have to ask for donations and report back to their supporters at all. If people don't understand their issues and support their work, it's not the nonprofit's fault. It's because the community is full of idiots who just don't get it. In other words, nonprofit marketing is a waste of precious time they need to spend on real work, so why bother? Although I run into an organization with this attitude from time to time, thankfully they are rare, in part because once they run out of seed money, they implode.

Grandma-Knows-Best

Unlike the Curmudgeonly Uncle, Grandma-Knows-Best thinks you deserve a gift, but she doesn't really care what's on your list because she knows what's best for you. You are going to get an electric toothbrush if you are lucky, and a scarf she knitted if you aren't. Either way, that present is going to be good for you, whether you like it or not.

Grandma-Knows-Best nonprofits write newsletters full of articles about the organization, its activities, and its issues, with little regard for who actually reads the newsletter. In fact, they aren't even sure who's on the newsletter list, and it really doesn't matter. Knowing wouldn't change the content. They decide what goes into the newsletter – end of story. I'd say about a third of nonprofit newsletters fall into this category.

Slacker Brother

He knows he is supposed to get you something, but he doesn't want to put any thought or effort into it, let alone money, so he is going to regift to you something he got for his birthday.

Slacker Brother nonprofits fill their publications with articles from other sources, with little original content, because it's quick and easy and they want to check the newsletter off the to-do list. Some of it may be helpful, but it's a toss-up most of the time. About a tenth of the newsletters I see fall into this category.

Well-Meaning Parent

They know what you really want and also what you need. They give you a mix. You'll get that fun new game you wanted, because they want you to be happy, but you'll also get something they think you need, like socks and underwear.

Well-Meaning Parent nonprofits are those who are sincerely interested in understanding their community and try to speak to their interests and values in most of their communications, but they can't quite let go of all of the organization-centered information. The boring "message from the executive director" column, for example, is still at the front of the print newsletter. Making sure that all the various programs get equal billing in the newsletter is more important to them than focusing on the programs that interest supporters the most. About half of nonprofit newsletters fall into this category.

Cool Aunt

She gets it right every time. She asks you what's on your wish list, or asks others what you are into these days. You can't wait to open her present. You'd open it the second it arrived if you could.

Cool Aunt nonprofits know who they are communicating with and are constantly checking in with their community, whether by talking to them directly, listening through social media, or staying on top of larger trends through research. They regularly adjust the content of their communications, and even their publishing schedule, to be relevant to their community right now. Their donors and supporters can tell that these nonprofits care what they think and are grateful for their participation. As much as possible, their newsletters are tools for not only delivering content but also sparking conversation and interaction. The donors and supporters love these nonprofits in return. About a tenth of the newsletters I see come from Cool Aunt organizations.

Do the print and online publications you produce and the conversations you have on social media sites feel like gifts to your participants and supporters, or are they simply what you think they need or what you want to give them for your own self-centered reasons? Start working your way down the continuum toward the Cool Aunt, and eventually you'll be the favorite nonprofit on everyone's list.

STRIVE FOR SHORTER, MORE FREQUENT COMMUNICATIONS IN MULTIPLE PLACES

In general, most nonprofits aren't communicating frequently enough. Instead, they save up content and then send too much all at once. A better approach is to send less content, but more frequently.

Finding the right rhythm is a function of your ability to produce high-quality relevant content and your capacity to send it out regularly.

You also need to understand for yourself what your organization can reasonably expect to produce on a regular schedule given your resource constraints. So much of successful nonprofit marketing depends on the creation of great content, including articles for your newsletter, website, blog, press releases, and so on, as well as images and video. How much great content do you think you can create and how often? How much you communicate, when, and where is the product of both elements: what they will find relevant and what you can realistically produce.

If your content is low quality, but you don't send much, you will likely be ignored. If your content is low quality but you send a lot, you'll be tagged as spam and people will unsubscribe.

On the other hand, if you produce high-quality content, but you don't send it very often, you'll be underperforming, because you simply aren't giving the recipients enough opportunities to see the content and to act on it. Remember, we all need to see a message many times before we are likely to act upon it.

The best case? You produce a lot of high-quality content and communicate frequently and consistently. This gives your supporters ample opportunity to engage with your content. And even when they don't, because they recognize it as high quality, they likely won't unsubscribe or label you as spam.

Just how often is enough? If you don't know where to begin, I suggest that you contact your supporters an average of twice a month via direct mail or email or a combination. Weekly is even better. To this, you'll add your social media messaging, which is often daily or every other day on average.

See how it goes and what kind of response you get. Then adjust these schedules to match what's best for your organization and your supporters.

WRITE LIKE THE SMART, PASSIONATE HUMAN BEING YOU ARE (NOT THE WONKY JARGON DROID YOU SOUND LIKE NOW)

People give to and support nonprofits for highly subjective and personal reasons. Your supporters get something deeply personal out of their affiliation with your organization as a donor, volunteer, or advocate. So why would your response back to these passionate people be institutional, monolithic, and completely objective?

You need to break out of the "501(c)(3) speaks to the masses" writing mode if you want your communications to be successful. Good nonprofit writing is personal, informal, direct, friendly, and, when appropriate, funny – in other words, it's human. Although there are certainly times when the newsy, facts-only journalistic style can work, the overwhelming majority of your communications with supporters should be much friendlier. Here are a few tips:

- Speak directly to your reader by calling them "you" and refer to yourself and your nonprofit as "we" or "I."

- Use bylines. Let your readers know who is writing each article.

- Make people central to your content. Include your staff, donors, volunteers, clients, and others by name in your articles.

- Tell stories in your newsletters to engage your donors in your work, to reinforce their giving decisions, to inspire them to do more, and to encourage more word-of-mouth marketing on your behalf.

- Include headshots or photos with people. Show your readers who's talking and who you are talking about.

Your supporters give their time, talents, and gifts with passion for your cause. They are part of the family. Write to them that way.

REMEMBER TO REPURPOSE YOUR CONTENT

As any successful media mogul knows, you never put your content out there just once. You are constantly reusing it and making it available in many different places at many different times. If you are struggling to produce enough high-quality content to communicate weekly or twice a month, odds are that you aren't fully employing these content repurposing techniques – and you should be.

Use a different channel. If you've written a blog post, is there something you can do with that content elsewhere? Many times your blog, your website, your email newsletter, and your print newsletter will feed each other and you'll remix between those channels. Three short blog posts can be combined into one longer newsletter article. You can use a top 10 list you published in your email newsletter as a starting point for a video script.

Edit for a different segment. Also think about your different segment and how you can put a slightly different spin on existing content to make it more relevant to a different group. Often it's as simple as rewriting the headlines and the opening sentence.

Make short stuff longer. If you started with a 200-word blog post or even a quick tweet or Facebook update, flesh that out into a newsletter article by adding some examples. Add more descriptive details, get quotes from people, or share opposing points of view.

Make long stuff shorter. Pull the headline and use it as a status update. Reduce your paragraphs to bullet points. Publish a teaser and link to the longer piece.

Change the lead. Simply start the article in a whole new way. Move something that was lower down in the article to the top. If you didn't use a quote in the first paragraph before, use one now. Open with a trend or other big-picture explanation.

Change the perspective. You can also change the perspective, so you tell the same story, but from a slightly different point of view. Maybe you're talking about three people with whom your organization has worked and you're emphasizing one of them. Tell the same basic story, but emphasize another person in the story this time.

Change the format. Start with live audio and record it as a podcast, video, or webinar recording. Have the recorded audio transcribed. Pull text from that. If you've written a how-to article, turn it into a top 10 list. If you've written a top 10 list about how to do something, rewrite it as an opinion piece or a review.

IMPROVE YOUR SOCIAL MEDIA ENGAGEMENT

Think about the conversations you have through social media as akin to a big cocktail party with lots of influential and interesting people in the room – a prime location for professional networking. To get the most out of that party, you have to work the room, but in a fairly specific way.

For example, you don't want to stand on a chair and start yelling over everyone's heads. You don't want to walk up to each person, interrupt their conversations, and thrust your business cards in their faces. People will first glare at you and then turn away completely. The same applies in social media. It's not about you. It's about, as Chris Brogan and Julien Smith say in *Trust Agents*, being "one of us." To be successful at a cocktail party and in social media, you have to see yourself and behave as a *member* of the community you are trying to reach.

You do so by sharing interesting information, being helpful to others, giving praise where it's due, and inspiring people with your stories. It doesn't hurt to have a good sense of humor too. There are always a few groups at big cocktail parties that everyone seems to gravitate toward. You can usually identify them by the number of people standing around spellbound by the person in the center (or by the raucous laughter). You become the person people gravitate to online by being a helpful, friendly expert, while remaining "one of us."

Even if you are chatting with just one person at the bar and you aren't sure whether others are listening in or not, you still have to keep up your end of the conversation. Don't stare at the bottles on the wall or, worse, try to catch a glimpse of yourself in the mirror beyond while someone is talking to you. In social media, that means not only putting out your own updates, but responding to those posted by others. Don't just sit and stare at your own work.

If you aren't already doing so, give some of the following social media engagement techniques a try. While social media is constantly changing, the following approaches produced high engagement in 2019–2020. And yet many nonprofits weren't using them, according to the *2020 Nonprofit Communications Trends Report*.

About half (53 percent) of nonprofits said they manage an active Facebook Group. Facebook is reinvesting heavily into Groups and Mark Zuckerberg has said that he expects much of the future user activity on Facebook to take place in private Groups.

Less than half (42 percent) of nonprofits post to Instagram Stories at least weekly. Instagram Stories are the fastest growing social media format in 2020. Several social media industry insiders believe that the Stories format will soon overtake the more traditional Newsfeed format as the primary way people use social media.

Only a quarter of nonprofits (25 percent) actively encourage communications via Facebook Messenger or a chat bot. In addition to Groups, Facebook is also encouraging users to connect with brands via Messenger as a more private communications channel. Even if you don't use Messenger specifically, it's extremely likely that you'll need to use an instant messaging or chat program with supporters, and that will likely include a bot to help automate some of those conversations.

Only 17 percent of nonprofits say they actively encourage people to create Facebook Fundraisers for their nonprofits. We see all of the problems with Facebook Fundraisers from the nonprofit's perspective. We hope Facebook will work with nonprofits to address some of those concerns. However, there is no arguing with the ease of giving for donors.

Just 13 percent say they livestream video at least monthly. Video posts are by far the most engaging content on social media, and live video streams are watched even longer than recorded videos.

These are the social media tactics that work and that social media companies themselves are investing in and banking on to keep users coming back every day.

If you are frustrated with lackluster results on social media, it's time to re-evaluate your strategy. You might consider going all-in with at least one of these engaging tactics.

THE EMAIL ENGAGEMENT CRISIS

I'm generally not a "the sky is falling" alarmist person by nature. But email engagement is one area where I believe we in the nonprofit sector need to pull the alarm. Nonprofits that ignore email engagement and list management best practices will soon find that what used to be an effective communications tool has become utterly unreliable and perhaps even useless.

Why? Because, as we saw from Neely's story at the beginning of this chapter, if you don't manage your email marketing for engagement, your deliverability will go down. That's the email jargon for "your emails will go straight to the spam folder." It's time to stop worrying so much about whether your subject line sounds spammy and start worrying about how you manage your mailing list.

EveryAction's *2019 Email Deliverability Study* estimated that the nonprofit sector could be losing almost $100 million in donations because appeals are going into spam folders. In its 2019 end-of-year fundraising season wrap-up, the consulting and research firm M+R reported that email deliverability was a big problem, with many nonprofits struggling to get their email appeals into inboxes. In their 2018 year-end analysis, they found that nonprofits who saw their list size drop year-over-year (because they actively managed their lists, dropping the unengaged) also saw better returns: a 26 percent improvement in response rate and a 2 percent improvement in email revenue.[2]

A basic tenet of email engagement and deliverability is to only mail to people who demonstrate that they want your content by continuing to open it. It doesn't take much to be considered "engaged." While there isn't a hard and fast rule at this time, most email service providers consider a subscriber engaged if they have opened at least one email in the last three to six months.

When a subscriber has stopped opening emails after a designated amount of time, you should send them a re-engagement series of emails to try to get them to open an email again. If they still don't open an email, you should stop emailing them (or at a minimum, limit the number of emails you send in the future.)

In the *2020 Nonprofit Communications Trends Report*, we found very few nonprofits had adopted these best practices.

A little over half of nonprofits were implementing email re-engagement campaigns, although they were often waiting too long to do them. We found that 12 percent of nonprofits considered someone unengaged at three months or less and therefore ready for a re-engagement campaign. Another 15 percent set this mark at six months, and 27 percent set it at 12 months. The remaining 46 percent of nonprofits surveyed do not send email re-engagement campaigns.

Unfortunately, even some nonprofits who are running re-engagement campaigns stop there and fail to scale back or stop emailing unengaged subscribers. A whopping 77 percent of nonprofits said that they never cut back the number of emails they send to unengaged subscribers, with 69 percent saying they never stop emailing, even if the subscriber is clearly no longer engaged. This is incredibly dangerous behavior.

Some nonprofits are trying, of course. But their standards for when to slow or stop emailing are far outside the email industry benchmark of three to six months. Only 4 percent of nonprofits cut back sending after three months of no engagement, with another 5 percent cutting back at six months of no engagement. Another 13 percent cut back at somewhere between one to three years.

Removing someone from the mailing list entirely is even harder for nonprofits to implement relatively quickly. Just 4 percent of nonprofits said they would stop emailing someone entirely if they hadn't engaged in six months. Eleven percent of nonprofits are using the 12-month mark, with another 16 percent stopping email at some point between 18 months and three years.

It's just not good enough. You must stop emailing people who never open your emails. Otherwise, you have no one to blame but yourself when your email engagement rates continue to plummet.

CONCLUSION: CONVERSATION DOES PAY OFF

If you've worked for long in nonprofit fundraising (or in venture capital, a field in which funds must also be raised), you'll recall hearing the saying, "Ask for money and you get advice. Ask for advice and you get money." Investments in nonprofits and businesses alike start with respectful conversations, often with one person asking for the advice or input of the other. Just as friendly chats at cocktail parties can lead to incredible connections that pay off big in the weeks, months, and years to come, the same is true in social media, email, and other communications channels that you use to stay in touch with your community.

Empower Your Fans to Build More Support

In March 2020, COVID-19 turned the world upside down. The University of California at Berkeley, like every university, closed the campus and many students returned home. UC Berkeley employees struggled to figure out what to do next and how to continue to support the broader campus community. That included Amy Cranch, principal editor for university development and alumni relations, and her colleague in external relations, Maya Goehring-Harris.

"We became consumed for months with how to celebrate and communicate with the graduating Class of 2020," said Amy. As the uncertainty around COVID-19 grew and shifted, so did the decision about holding an in-person graduation ceremony, which 30,000 to 50,000 people usually attend.

Amy knew it was important to listen to their students. "When schools across the nation began canceling their graduations or moving them online, often without getting students' input, they protested. We wanted to make sure our students had a say," said Amy. The chancellor sent an email survey completed by nearly 3,200 students, setting the stage for how to move forward. While the students overwhelmingly preferred an in-person ceremony, at that point, Amy knew they needed to work on different approaches.

One of those approaches was creating Cal Grad Day, a social media campaign to solicit love letters from alumni, parents, faculty, staff, and others to the Class of 2020. The action date was May 16, 2020, the original commencement date. Using a toolkit provided by the team, more than 1,200 people participated in Twitter and Instagram, blowing their goal of 600 posts away.

But something even bigger was underway within the Cal community. Shortly after shelter in place began in mid-March, a small group of students and alumni began rebuilding the campus in meticulous, startling detail in Minecraft, the video game. They called the virtual campus Blockeley. "That handful of builders grew to hundreds, and the idea arose to recreate commencement in the virtual Minecraft stadium. A core group submitted a formal proposal to the university to sponsor it, and Chancellor Carol Christ wholeheartedly embraced the idea," said Amy.

While the students remained the visionaries and key planners for this unofficial ceremony, Amy and Maya joined the team to provide counsel and support on a variety of items. They worked with students on crafting the ceremony; securing keynote speakers; writing and prerecording speeches for the chancellor and other speakers; creating avatars; determining how to live stream the event on other platforms; communicating with parents, the media, and other audiences; and helping run a myriad of backend logistics required to pull off what became – as far as Amy knows – the world's first-ever university commencement in Minecraft.

"While we still haven't been able to honor the Class of 2020 in a way it deserves, we are exceptionally proud of what we did to ensure they were not forgotten amid the overwhelming challenges of a pandemic," said Amy.

Hundreds of graduating seniors participated in the mock ceremony. It was such a success that the Minecraft server at Blockeley.com will now be used for virtual campus tours and perhaps other events. Nostalgic graduates can also visit when they miss being on campus.

Amy, Maya, and the rest of the UC Berkeley employees involved in Blockeley could have refused to help the students because it wasn't a staff idea and they weren't in control. But Amy and Maya understand the power of a highly engaged community and the amazing things that can happen when you empower that community to make exciting things happen. This too, is part of your role as a nonprofit communicator.

As you get to know your supporters, you'll find that some small percentage of them – perhaps 5 percent or maybe as much as 20 percent – are not just average supporters, but truly big fans who want do whatever they can to help you. In this chapter, we'll look what makes someone a fan, how to make them feel even better about your organization, and ways to encourage them to build even more support for your cause.

IDENTIFY YOUR WALLFLOWERS, BUDDIES, AND FANS

The people who make up your various lists of supporters (mailing lists, blog subscribers, social networking friends, and so on) usually fall into one of three categories: wallflowers, buddies, or fans.

Wallflowers. They are in touch with you, but prefer to keep to themselves. They subscribe to your newsletter or blog and wish you well, but they don't actively participate by volunteering, donating, or advocating for your cause. In online parlance, they are lurkers, which sounds negative, but isn't. It just means they are the quiet ones who pay attention to what's going on but don't actively participate. When you see that your email newsletter is being opened by only 15 percent of the people receiving it, you may wonder who the other 85 percent are. They are your wallflowers: they want to stay on your list, but they only occasionally read what you send them.

The conventional wisdom of "participation inequality"[1] is that lurkers make up 90 percent of online communities. More recent research suggests that percentage is too high, and that higher percentages of people are falling into the next two categories, people who contribute sometimes or most of the time.

Buddies. Buddies like your organization and what you do. They sometimes volunteer time, donate money, or attend your events. They'll sometimes comment on your blog posts and occasionally forward your newsletter to their friends. But if you don't ask them to act, they probably won't do it on their own. Buddies, or intermittent contributors, traditionally make up 9 percent of online communities, and often more in smaller, more active communities. They represent part of the 15 percent of nonprofit e-newsletters that do get opened. When you ask people on your email list to take an action, they'll do so one to five times per year, and as a group will represent two-thirds of all actions taken.

Fans. Fans regularly connect with you and your cause and spread the word to others without being asked to do so, because they love what you do and being associated with your good cause. Although they are relatively few compared to the size of your buddy and wallflower groups, they are your most loyal volunteers, donors, and advocates and are therefore incredibly powerful. Fans, or heavy contributors, make up just 1 percent of online communities. In active and highly engaged groups, that 1 percent can grow to more like 20 percent, or even 30 percent, although this is rare. They will nearly always be a part of the group that's responsible for the 2 percent click-through rate for nonprofit e-newsletters.

They are also the 7 percent of people on your email list who take six or more of your requested actions, representing a third of the total actions taken. You'll sometimes see your fans called patrons, evangelists, or über-friends.

You can *convert wallflowers into buddies* by continuing to share positive news, offering helpful resources, and building up trust in your organization over time. Make it easy to get involved by offering a variety of options that don't require a long-term commitment. Then when you happen to mention a program or opportunity that matches their values perfectly, many of them will step up.

You can *convert buddies into fans* by thanking them personally for what they do and reporting back on the difference they are making. Always reinforce that when they do take some kind of action, it really does make a difference. Think about ways to reward your buddies, by offering them some kind of special status or publicly acknowledging them at in-person events and through your social networking connections (such as retweeting or replying on Twitter or liking or commenting on Facebook).

However, for a small but very important group, this is only the beginning. For your most interested and active supporters – your biggest fans – you need to do more than stay in touch. You need to fully engage them in your work and reward them for their support by making them feel like part of the team. It takes a personal, conversational, one-on-one touch that can happen offline, online, or both.

You want to turn casual supporters into true friends – friends who advocate for your cause and organization within their own networks and beyond, who support you financially, and who help you in ways you never imagined. You want to create bonds between these friends and build a strong and extensive social network of people who are there for you. But it's a two-way street, and that means you need to be there for them too.

WHAT MAKES SOMEONE A FAN?

The qualities of the biggest fans of your organization are not all that different from what makes someone a big fan of a sports team.

There's an emotional connection. Your cause touches something deep inside of your supporters and makes them willing to do anything for you. Sports fans paint their faces and wear outlandish costumes. Your fans might do something many would consider equally outlandish, like hosting a party in their own home, inviting all of their friends over, paying for the food, and then giving you the floor to talk about your cause while they ask their friends to empty their wallets. To top it off, they'll write a big check themselves, one of many over the course of their relationship with your organization. Or they might do the online equivalent, like emailing all of their friends about you. They might call in a big favor, but on your behalf instead of their own.

They believe they matter. Your biggest fans believe their actions will have a real impact – and you can't do it without them. Sports fans bring signs and cheer and chant, because they believe it will inspire their teams to play better. Your biggest fans also believe that their support really matters and that they are making it possible for you to do your best and to bring about real changes to make the world a better place.

They want to belong. Your biggest fans want to feel like they are part of something bigger than themselves. Sports fans dress in the team colors and do the wave. Your biggest fans also want to feel like they are part of something bigger by seeing how their individual contributions, combined with others, can produce something amazing. Many of the challenges in the world today seem impossible to address as an individual. But when individuals become part of your team, they can see how their small contribution adds up to so much more. Make them feel like they really are valued members of your team.

It feels good. Your biggest fans also get a "helper's high" – a feeling of well-being and happiness that's been scientifically documented in volunteers. Sports fans party in the stands, hanging out with friends and having a good time. Your fans get a boost too, because giving feels good, both emotionally and physically.

GIVE YOUR BIGGEST FANS THE PERSONAL TOUCH

A supporter's interest in helping your organization always starts with their values, not yours. People support nonprofits who reinforce their own value systems. That means you need to pay attention to what they specifically care about and start there as you develop a relationship with your supporters.

If you operate multiple programs, for example, it's likely that your biggest fans care much more about the success of one of those programs than all the others, because that one program touches them in some very personal way. Don't assume that a supporter who is investing many hours a week to make your "puppy manners class" for new dog owners a success will be equally enthused about fundraising to build a new playroom for cats awaiting adoption.

I made an unsolicited donation to a children's health charity after watching a news program about the incredible work they were doing in the Gulf Coast helping children whose lives had been turned upside down by Hurricanes Katrina and Rita. My donation was designated on their website donation form specifically for this program in the Gulf Coast. I might very well have become a lifelong supporter of the group, except the next solicitation they sent me was about reducing childhood asthma in New York City. They disconnected me from my original reason for giving, and I disconnected from them as a donor.

Your biggest fans deserve special, personal treatment. Even a small organization can provide personal treatment to some percentage of its biggest fans. Even if you can't get to everyone, start with some of them. Ask board members or other volunteer leaders to help by playing the role of "ambassador" to your biggest fans. Ask each person to personally call a short list of key supporters a few times a year, to send handwritten thank-you notes, to write personal notes on the top of their newsletters, or to forward an email about something in the news that they believe the fan will find particularly interesting.

When you treat your cause's fans like true friends, amazing things can happen. Consider the experience that John Bell, an experienced major donor fundraiser, had with one of his long-time donors, an older woman we'll call Ann Smith.

Ann's ancestors came from a particular county in the North Carolina mountains that John knows well, and he and Ann share a love of history and vernacular architecture. John realized that another nonprofit group he belonged to was hosting a fundraiser at a pioneer home that was once in Ann's family. Ann had not seen the home in many years and was thrilled when John invited her to attend the fundraiser with him, including driving her there.

Ann also serves on a local college's library board. When John was traveling through the area where Ann's ancestors had come from, he noticed a history book about that county in a local bookstore. John bought the book and sent it to the college library for their collection. The library placed a nameplate in the book that reads "Given in honor of Ann Smith" and sent a card to Ann acknowledging John's gift.

When John saw an article in the *New York Times* that reminded him of an issue that Ann had once worked on in another state, he cut out the article and sent it to her. In one of their conversations, Ann informed John of a large six-figure bequest she would be making to his nonprofit.

John didn't bring Ann to the event, buy the book in her honor, and send her the newspaper clipping with any expectation that she would include his organization in her estate plans. He did all these things because he values Ann not only as a nonprofit donor but also as a friend with interests far beyond the cause he represents. He's invested time in that friendship, getting to know Ann as a person. If he hadn't really paid attention to who Ann is and listened to her, he wouldn't have been able to make any of these heartfelt personal gestures that helped build this friendship.

John has raised funds for a civil rights foundation, an AIDS services organization, a health clinic, a homeless shelter, conservation groups, and low-income housing, and he has many similar stories to share, as do most successful development directors. "It's morally repugnant and cynical – and ultimately futile – to try to make donors give just by being kind, or generous, or considerate," says John. "Like in all relationships, practice the Golden Rule. A donor relationship will grow stronger if you think more about the other person than about yourself."

ENCOURAGE WORD-OF-MOUTH MARKETING AND REFERRALS

When people are talking about the issues you work on, will your name come up in conversation?

You'll want to be on the tip of the tongue of experts in your communities, whether geographic, professional, or topical. Recommendations from personal acquaintances remain the most trusted form of communication. What our friends, even mere acquaintances, tell us matters – a lot.

Do your best to make sure that when people ask your buddies and fans for a recommendation related to your mission, they mention your name. Some people are more likely than others to be asked for recommendations on a particular issue. If you want to know about environmentally friendly household cleaners, you are more likely to ask someone who drives a Prius or tends an organic vegetable garden than someone who drives a gas guzzler or sprays chemicals on their lawn.

Building up your word-of-mouth referrals takes time, but it can be a very powerful form of marketing for nonprofits. In fact, it's probably the best form of marketing because it's free (or relatively cheap) and it's trusted.

The Word of Mouth Marketing Association defines the basics of word-of-mouth marketing as:

- Educating people about your products and services
- Identifying people most likely to share their opinion
- Providing tools that make it easier to share information
- Studying how, where, and when opinions are being shared
- Listening and responding to supporters, detractors, and neutrals[2]

Using this list as a guide, think about ways you can encourage your current supporters – especially your buddies and fans – to tell others about your organization.

Let's say we work on animal issues in our community. If we run a public animal shelter, then we'll use the shelter address as our primary home base. In all of our marketing campaigns, we'll always make sure our street address is clear.

But what if we don't have a facility and instead are a network of people who provide foster care for animals until we can find homes for them? Even though we have a P.O. box, we aren't going to emphasize that. Instead, we'll connect with people primarily through our website, so that's what we'll promote as our primary home base.

Which directories should we be listed in? What would people do if they either found or lost a pet? Who would they call for recommendations? Here are some of the likely people and places our nonprofit should be in touch with, so they know who we are and the best way for people to reach us.

Government agencies. Most local governments have a department that handles animal control issues. They may respond only in emergency situations, but we'd want whoever answers that phone number to know we exist and to offer us as a resource for people calling about lost or found pets.

Professionals who work with animals. We should contact every veterinary office, pet shop, dog walker, pet sitter, and groomer in our area and keep them updated on how we can help their customers.

Other animal charities. We should contact every other animal-related group we know, even if they don't deal with cats and dogs, including equestrian groups. Remember, if I've lost a dog, and I have the choice to ask a friend for suggestions, I'll pick the friend who has horses over one who has no pets at all.

BE CLEAR ABOUT THE BEST WAYS FOR PEOPLE TO HELP

Some of your fans will prefer to give money, others will prefer to give time. Some of your fans will be outgoing and love meeting new people in person; others will prefer to network online. The fastest way to lose a fan is to insist that there is only one way to offer support – your way. You'll burn out your supporters if you ask them to do things they don't really want to do. Instead, create a flexible, diverse list of ways that your fans can help you, and let each person decide what's best for her. Just as every member of your staff is a marketer (like it or not), think of all of your fans as special envoys of your marketing team to the rest of the world.

"How can someone who loves this organization help you?" When I ask a nonprofit this question, I'm always a little surprised to get a blank stare in return. Or worse: answers that involve stuffing envelopes, filing paperwork, and other mundane tasks. If someone says, "How can I help you?" always be ready with at least three options. These should change given what's going on in your office, the time of year, and what's needed most. Once a month, sit down with your staff and come up with your wish list for volunteer help. Then make sure your fans know what's on that list so they can help you find the right people. Use a question from a supporter, like "How can I help?" to start a conversation. Reply with a question of your own: What do you enjoy doing or what are you interested in learning more about?

Even if all of your programmatic needs are met, every nonprofit can suggest two opportunities that help market your cause: friendraising and peer-to-peer or microfundraising.

ENCOURAGE YOUR FANS TO FRIENDRAISE

Even if you don't need volunteers in the traditional sense, there's always something that people who care about your cause can do for you, and it's called friendraising. Fundraising is scary to many people, but friendraising is easier. Simply ask your big fan to tell five of their friends about you in whatever way is most comfortable for them. They can talk about your nonprofit over lunch or coffee or on social media.

Research and practical experience show that we are most effectively persuaded to do something when our friends, family, and colleagues are the ones doing the talking. Here are some of the tools you can offer fans to help with friendraising:

- Create content about your issues that fans can freely use in their own blogs, social media profiles, newsletters, and so on. Think about how-to articles, success stories, top ten lists, question-and-answer interviews, and other favorite formats.

- Find a way to solve a problem that people care about. Share it with your fans so they can share it with others.

- Give fans the missing resources or tools they need to make a difference on their own. What's missing? Ask your fans! They'll tell you.

- Give them step-by-step help on how to donate online, upload videos, and the like. Even if they don't need this help themselves, people in their networks probably will. Help your fans be helpful to their own friends.

ENCOURAGE YOUR FANS TO FUNDRAISE

The thought of asking someone for hundreds or thousands of dollars scares many people. On the other hand, asking for $5 or $10, especially for a good cause, is much more doable. The nonprofit jargon for this concept is "microphilanthropy" or "peer-to-peer fundraising" and it's been going on for decades as friends "sponsor" friends in events like 5K walks. Peer-to-peer fundraising now happens constantly on social media through Facebook Fundraisers and on other social media sites.

Here are a few ways to encourage your fans to raise money from their friends on your behalf:

Share their own story. Why does your fan support your nonprofit? That's a story they should share with their own friends. Making the cause personal will help encourage people to donate.

Provide easy software to collect and track donations. The number of peer-to-peer giving platforms has exploded. These software companies make it easy for individuals and teams to fundraise by allowing them to create their own profiles and fundraising pages, to send email and social media messages directly from the platform, and to track success on leaderboards.

Encourage them to ask for specific amounts. People who ask for specific amounts tend to raise more money.

Provide progress reports to your fans. Help your fundraisers see how they are part of something much bigger by providing updates on how the larger campaign is going.

APPROACH NEW FRIENDS OF FRIENDS

Your biggest fans spread the word for you and even collect money for you. Now how do you bring those new people they've introduced to your cause into your community and transform them from wallflowers to buddies to fans? The standard advice is to come up with a cultivation campaign that introduces these new people to the organization over time and encourages them to become directly involved with the nonprofit as a volunteer or donor, as if they had discovered the organization on their own.

The problem is that this treats the person we'll call the Original Fan like some kind of inconvenient or spent middleman. For many nonprofits, the Original Fan is anything but a middleman; instead, he or she is more like a gatekeeper or nightclub bouncer. It's only through the Original Fan that the nonprofit will have access to those people and their wallets.

Most national organizations with widely understood or broadly supported missions should probably go ahead and try to establish direct relationships with all of those friends of friends. But nonprofits with specific geographic limitations or niche missions (for example, diseases that affect relatively few people) should move forward much more carefully and deliberately, checking to see just how likely it is that the friends of friends will actually convert into long-term, direct donors. Many of these friends of friends will be just one-time givers, and that's OK.

For example, I donated money to a food bank in New Jersey because my friend Nancy asked me to as part of her birthday celebration. Although I certainly support the mission of food banks in general, I live in North Carolina. Nancy is the sole reason that I donated to this food bank in New Jersey. No matter how many newsletters or appeal letters the New Jersey food bank might send me in the future, it is extremely unlikely that I will ever give them another dime.

Unless, of course, Nancy – the Original Fan – asks me to.

That's why when the executive director of a local HIV/AIDS group for whom I fundraised as part of my birthday celebration asked me whether she should add the names of my donating friends to her prospect database, I told her no.

I served on the board of directors of this particular organization, so that's why I was asked. (I doubt that few Original Fans are consulted in this way at all – which is part of the problem.) Instead, I asked her to send a thank-you note directly to my donating friends and invite them to sign up for the e-newsletter if they wanted to. I've asked her not to message these people again otherwise. As the Original Fan, I know these people are giving because of me, because I asked – not really because of the cause. Although I'm sure that everyone who donated supports the mission of the chosen organization, just as I support food banks, nearly all of the people who donated lived outside the geographic service area, and I believe it's extremely unlikely that they would give again on their own.

Unless, of course, I – the Original Fan – asked them to.

Although you should definitely spend some time coming up with cultivation strategies for friends of friends, it is equally important – and I'd argue *more* important for local or niche organizations – to develop strategies to keep your Original Fans fully engaged and willing to fundraise for you again and again.

The food bank and HIV/AIDS group don't need strategies to reach Nancy's friends and my friends; they need strategies to keep Nancy and me and all their other Original Fans happy with the organization and excited about its work so that we will continue to tap our networks on their behalf.

HOW TO HANDLE TROLLS

When you start listening to online conversations, you may find that not everything you hear is flattering. Although the majority of what you hear will probably be positive or neutral (unless you work on controversial social issues), you'll also run into the occasional and dreaded trolls.

Their motivation is to get attention. The troll will try to encourage chaos among your blog readers or social media followers by leaving rude comments, discouraging others from backing your cause, or riling you up with personal attacks. It's all with the same end in mind: "Notice me!" Whether you respond to them or ignore them depends on where the comment appears and what you believe the impact of the comment will be.

On your own blog and social channels, establish a comment policy. Let readers know exactly what you expect from them when they comment and what you will and will not condone. Keep it simple and stick to it.

When trolls strike, it's best not to feed them. If you can, ignore them. Trolls want attention, any kind of attention, so don't give it to them.

If you feel that you just can't ignore a comment, be careful in your response. Step away from the computer. Don't respond in anger, no matter how upsetting the comment is. Take some time and formulate a rational response. Disarm the crank by being positive. Find something of merit in what was said and start with that.

Before you get too worked up, be sure that what you are dealing with is actually a troll. Just because someone disagrees with you doesn't mean what they are saying isn't worthy of discussion. Diverging viewpoints among readers offer a great way to encourage conversation. Healthy, respectful debate is great for fostering community.

CONCLUSION: BUILD YOUR SOCIAL CAPITAL

The formal name for what you are building by giving your fans the personal touch is "social capital." Time, money, and skills are clearly valuable. But so is who you know and how willing they are to help you. Social capital is the willingness of people to help each other, and it can be viewed just like any other resource your nonprofit marketing program needs in order to succeed. This is especially true if you don't have enough time or money to run your marketing program the way you'd like.

Banking social capital is much easier than it sounds: be nice, be helpful, and most important, don't expect anything in return from those to whom you are nice and helpful. Do as much as you can for as wide a network as you can. Eventually, and most likely through circuitous routes you could never predict, you will be on the receiving end of equal amounts of kindness and aid – perhaps even more. Pay it forward, and it will make its way back around to you.

PART FOUR

Doing It Yourself Without Doing Yourself In

Every project or program, no matter how big or small, depends on a mixture of three ingredients: time, talent, and treasure. How much time can you devote to marketing, and how can you get others to offer their time? What can you do yourself, what other talent do you have on staff, and what tasks do you need to hire out? How much money do you have available and how should you spend it? We'll look at each of these three elements in this part. Chapter 15 provides tips on building your pool of talent, both from within yourself and by working with others. Chapter 16 reveals ways to market your good cause on a tight budget. Chapter 17 explores ways to get more done in less time.

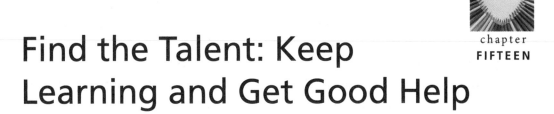

Find the Talent: Keep Learning and Get Good Help

Corinna Wagner, the marketing manager of ADRA Austria, a faith-based international nonprofit based in Vienna, has been on a journey to professionalize the communications and fundraising work at her organization.

"I decided to start with myself and become the professional that our local organization needed and also the worldwide network may need," said Corinna. She started by completing a BA in business marketing and continued with an MA in strategic marketing.

As she learned about the field, she brought ideas into her organization, and step-by-step, they began to adopt a series of best practices in communications and fundraising, including everything from better database software to segmenting and personalization. "This resulted in steadier donation income. Donations were increasing from year to year instead of going up and down," said Corinna.

As a result of some early successes, the organization began paying for training and coaching for staff. "The organized approach to learning through both studying for a degree and the coaching program helped me and others overcome the paralysis of having too much information," said Corinna. "We are now working more strategically, doing what brings us forward, and also making tough decisions to drop much-loved things that we now see are barriers to moving forward."

Showing her leadership the difference between newer campaigns where they implemented best practices and past campaigns where they didn't helped demonstrate that the investments in training were worth it. "They were more confident because they knew we now had the core competency within the organization, and we knew how to choose the right training or partners to work with, and how to implement what was taught in courses," said Corinna. "And after the first successful year-end appeal developed under the coaching, we had an increase of donations worth four times what we had paid for the coaching."

As you can see from Corinna's example, professional development is essential to growing your nonprofit's effectiveness. But marketing in the nonprofit world can mean different things to different people, which means your job description may vary significantly from someone with the same title at a nonprofit down the street. Do you write the newsletter? Do you have control over the website design? Are you responsible for fundraising? Are you the spokesperson for the nonprofit? Do you have a say in programmatic design and implementation decisions, or do program people work with you only when they need "outreach"?

No matter what exactly you are responsible for, nonprofit marketing requires a complicated skill set that's hard to find all in one person. It's a tough job.

In this chapter, we'll look at what you can do to build your own skills and how to delegate marketing tasks to others. We'll also look at empowering volunteers and hiring others to assist you. Get used to asking for help. You are going to need it.

BUILD YOUR OWN SKILLS

While you look for help from within your organization, you should also look at ways to improve your own skill set. If you are a marketing department of one or a do-it-all-yourself executive director, it's especially important that you use as many of the following strategies as you can to develop your skills.

Where to begin? We know from the *2019 Nonprofit Communications Trends Report* that nonprofit communicators say they are most skilled at:

- Creating relevant and engaging messaging
- Copywriting
- Leading communications decision making
- Public speaking

In the *2020 Nonprofit Communications Trends Report*, nonprofit communicators said they were most interested in building skills in these areas:

- Social media management
- Video production
- Graphic design

- Writing and storytelling
- Team management and planning
- Analytics and measuring success

Regardless of the specific topics you want to pursue, think about where you are now and where you'd like to be. For example, where can you move from knowledge to proficiency to mastery? I recommend the following five-step approach to building your own professional development plan.

Step 1: Create a Plan and Start Reading

The first step is to actually create a plan for yourself. Be methodical about it. You have to be strategic about what enters your brain! You have so much to read and so many webinars to attend. Sort through and filter your options based on what you really want to learn.

I suggest that you start with at least 15 minutes of daily reading or listening to podcasts on your topics. Take notes as you go and review those insights weekly.

There's an incredible amount of assistance out there, especially with constantly changing technology and the ways in which marketers are using it, if you take the time to find it and read it. Take 15 minutes a day or an hour a week to close the door, turn off the phone, sit back, and read blogs or books like this one. No time for reading? Listen instead to any of the great podcasts or videos that several nonprofit marketing consultants and tech companies are producing on nonprofit communications and marketing.

I love this approach shared with me by Tiffany Nyklickova, an information specialist with Services in Action in Toronto, Canada. By profession, she specializes in organizing information in a way that is easy to receive, understand, and use.

Tiffany subscribes to many newsletters and podcasts, attends webinars, participates in book clubs, and generally keep her eyes and ears open to what others are doing. And she takes notes. Lots and lots of handwritten notes. But she didn't just leave the notes in a big pile never to be read again like most of us do.

"I decided to tackle the stack of notes, to summit the mountain of communication tips and tricks," said Tiffany. "I spread out the papers and started categorizing – story ideas, writing techniques, planning techniques, media specific observations, quotes, etc. I opened up Word, and copied every relevant idea onto the document, into categories. I read through and deleted duplicate or now unnecessary ideas. The document was four pages."

Now, when it's time to work on a specific type of communications, she starts by scrolling through her notes document. "It sparks ideas and motivation. I continue to add and delete notes as necessary," said Tiffany. "I no longer feel like I don't know what I don't know."

Step 2: Seek Out Specific Experiences

What can you do in your current position? What can you do in peer organizations or associations? What could you do as a volunteer? What can do on your own?

This is about trying new things and getting beyond your current comfort zone. You have to be willing to experiment in order to learn.

Where you can, I'm a big fan of using your children and pets as your personal guinea pigs. I blogged about my kids for our far-flung family and friends for a year before I started blogging professionally. My first photo and video uploads were of pets and kids. Play around for a while at home before you try it at work.

Step 3: Get Your Nonprofit on Board

You can learn only so much on your own. Many opportunities will be free, but you'll need to fill in the gaps with paid training. Identify the training you need most and justify it. Outline what you need to learn how to do, why, and how much it will cost. Talk about how you can engage others at the organization in your learning. C'mon, you are in marketing, so market the need for that training budget! Explain how your productivity and results will change as a result of learning a new skill.

Are you curious what other nonprofits offer in training budgets? We shared some data in the *2018 Nonprofit Communications Trends Report.*

One quarter (24 percent) of nonprofits spend zero dollars on staff professional development in a typical year. But that means the majority do provide a training budget. The average training budget per person is $1,001, excluding organizations that have budgets of $0. On average, 60 percent of survey participants said they received a moderate, a lot, or a great deal of training for their jobs.

We also found that as training budgets rise, so does communications effectiveness. In the most effective organizations, 66 percent say they have received a moderate amount of training or more. That falls to just 56 percent in less effective organizations. In the most effective organizations, 39 percent are satisfied with the level of training received. That drops to 28 percent in less effective organizations.

Step 4: Document Your Portfolio

As you gain experience, be sure to document the work you are proud of in a way that you control, such as your own personal website. Show progressions in your work: don't be embarrassed by older work. Just label the progression. It demonstrates your capacity to learn and grow, which is always a sought-after trait. Also think about ways you can showcase your work, such as guest blogging and speaking at conferences.

Step 5: Get Out There and Talk to Others

There are times when you need to hunker down and get "it" done, whatever it is. But don't cut out networking with others. If you find the right group of smart, experienced people to hang out with, they will save you incredible amounts of time. It's healthy for both you and your organization for you to mix and mingle with people who understand the work you do but who aren't working on the exact same thing day in and day out. You'll make new connections, pick up some tips, and get some great advice.

I encourage you to network with people at the same level of experience as you and also with others at different levels of experience. You'll learn from the ones with more experience, and you can help teach those with less experience. Teaching others reinforces what you have learned yourself.

In summary, create a professional development plan for yourself that is a mix of training, practical experience, and networking.

EVERYONE ON STAFF IS A MARKETER (LIKE IT OR NOT)

Everyone talks about work when they're outside the office, so everyone on your staff is marketing your organization in one way or another. That's why it's so important that you keep everyone updated on both the strategies and the tactics you are using. Share everything from press releases and newsletters to direct mail appeals with everyone on staff at the same time that these go public – and if possible before they go public. Ask staff to follow all of your social media channels. If information overload is a problem or other staff just aren't interested in reading what you produce, create a short weekly briefing email and send it on Monday mornings to all staff so they know what's going out this week.

If you take the time to talk to staff members about how vital their role is in reaching out to your supporters, you may be surprised at the marketing skills you find in your midst. Are there any good writers, designers, or proofreaders on staff? Staff who seem to know everyone? People who know different software or social media sites inside-out?

Sit down with the other staff and talk about what they are good at and how they would like to help you get the word out about the organization. Marketing can be scary for people who know nothing about it. You'll be perceived as an expert, whether you are or not. Be supportive and look for ways that you can help programmatic staff, as you ask them to help you.

DELEGATE MARKETING TASKS TO OTHERS

No matter how dedicated to your cause you may be, you are still human, and there are only so many hours in the day. Decide what only you can do and what you can ask others to do, even if it means you have to accept that they may approach the task in a different way. Delegate what you can, especially tasks that are too easy for you (meaning someone else who is probably paid less than you can do it) as well as tasks that are too hard for you (meaning you can pay for someone else's expertise and get the job done much more quickly). Look for opportunities to train others to help you and be willing to let go of control enough so that they can.

Before you can find others to help you, you should have some sense for what you need them to do. Content creation is an obvious place to start. Ask someone to be a guest columnist for ongoing publications like your newsletters, blog, and website. Find volunteers who are into writing, design, photography, and videography. Can they create templates for you or create evergreen content for your social media accounts? Does your tabletop display for conferences and fairs need to be updated?

Research is another time-consuming task that can be done by others. Ask volunteers or consultants to interview and write up stories about your clients and donors. Ask them to research which reporters in your area are covering various types of stories to update your press list. Ask them to collect bids for print jobs or event catering. Match your needs with what your volunteers genuinely enjoy doing.

Do you have a volunteer with an analytical mind? Ask them to dive into your website and email newsletter stats to identify positive and negative trends and to look for hidden gems of information you can use to improve your marketing program.

After other staff, the most obvious place to turn for help is your board of directors. Who on your board of directors has skills that can help you? Board members aren't likely to actually do the work for you long term, but they may be able to put you in touch with great contacts who can make your work life much easier. Board members can also offer perspectives you may be missing on staff. They may also be willing to invest time to help you get your systems set up, such as creating templates for an email newsletter or suggesting new strategies to reach particular target audiences.

Next, look for supportive volunteers who are interested in working with your cause because they care. Come up with some substantive projects that you can supervise, but that you don't have time to do yourself. Volunteers should be able to see the impact of their work, or to at least understand how it helps make your organization work more smoothly.

EMPOWER VOLUNTEERS SO THEY'LL COME BACK AGAIN

Time is precious – more precious than money in some ways – and that's what volunteers are giving you. You want to get something out of your volunteers, and they want to get something out of the experience too. Never forget that. Here are some key principles for ensuring that your volunteers will want to keep volunteering for you:

- *Set clear expectations.* If volunteers are creating content for you, spell out the approval process so they understand that you may ask them to make changes. Explain how what you are asking them to create fits into your larger content creation strategy. Give them a sense for the type of feedback they can expect from you.

- *Assume they'll get it right.* Don't hover. Be supportive by asking if they have questions or need help, but otherwise assume that your volunteers are smart, capable, and responsible people who will do their best for you. If they do get it wrong, be positive by pointing out what is right and gently moving on to areas that need to be changed. Always end the conversation on a positive note, expressing your gratitude for their help.

- *Be flexible.* You need to make sure that what your volunteers are doing is something you need done. At the same time, don't be too prescriptive. Offer some flexibility in how the work gets done. This is especially true in areas where style and quality can be highly subjective, like writing and design. Acknowledge your own style. As you edit an article, try not to replace your volunteer's personal style with your own. Also know the differences between rules and questions of style. Before you make lots of changes to your volunteer's words, be sure you can clearly explain which corrections are essential and which are optional. Your editorial style sheet will come in handy here!

- *Let them do what they love.* As much as possible, match tasks to what volunteers really enjoy doing. Your best volunteers will be those who are excited about the work and feel like they are personally gaining something from the experience.

- *Thank them and thank them again.* Share your gratitude for the help often. Remember, without them, either you'd be doing the work late at night or it wouldn't get done at all. Always remind your volunteers how important they are and about the real difference they are making.

HIRE CONSULTANTS AND FREELANCERS

When you don't have the important, creative skills you need on staff to accomplish your nonprofit marketing program, look for affordable freelancers and consultants to fill in the gaps. Ask yourself these seven questions before you hire a freelance creative professional, such as a writer, editor, graphic artist, or designer.

Before you start interviewing . . .

1. *What do I want a freelancer to do?* The more specific you can be about what you need, the better you'll be able to recruit a freelancer who can meet your needs. Most writers think in terms of word count or page count when estimating a job, so you should think that way too. How much writing do you need? How much research or interviewing will the writer need to do? How many drafts do you typically want to see?

2. *What is my ideal deadline, and what is the* real *deadline?* Most people want projects they are hiring out to be completed yesterday. Although it's fine

to suggest an ideal deadline when soliciting proposals from freelancers, know in your own mind how much play you have in your schedule. If the perfect candidate comes along, but can't meet your ideal deadline, for whatever reason, do you have enough cushion in your schedule to hire that person anyway?

3. *How much do I have to spend?* Rates for freelancers vary widely. In some respects, you do get what you pay for, but even among highly qualified and experienced freelancers you will still find a great deal of variability in rates. Know how much you have to spend ahead of time, so when you begin to evaluate proposals you can eliminate those that are far beyond your means. At the same time, you should also strongly consider eliminating proposals that seem exceedingly low – it's a hallmark of an inexperienced freelancer to charge way below market rate.

As you are interviewing . . .

4. *Is this freelancer a good listener?* Equally important as creative skills is the ability to listen to your needs and incorporate them into the project. Your projects will include many variables, such as audience, message, and tone, all of which require that you and the freelancer work together to get it right. You should treat this relationship as a partnership, which requires that you both listen well.

5. *Does this freelancer seem flexible?* Much of marketing is subjective. While some elements, such as correct grammar and word count, are objective, whether the piece meets your needs in terms of style is highly subjective. A good freelancer knows this and will work with you to get the style the way you want it, even if the first draft is way off.

Also, as the project progresses, you may very well change your mind about how you want an issue handled or what elements should be emphasized. Try to gauge whether the freelancer can "go with the flow" and adjust accordingly. Of course, you need to be willing to pay for extra drafts if you change the scope of work significantly.

6. *Do I like this freelancer's portfolio and client list?* Does the freelancer have experience with your type of project? Does the freelancer's list of clients relate to your organization in subject area, size, or some other meaningful measure? All professional freelancers should be able to provide samples

of their work (many will have online portfolios for you to peruse) and to give you a list of people they have worked for previously.

7. *How do this freelancer's other clients describe their relationships?* Yes, you should check references. Speaking directly with another client is one of the best ways to judge how well a freelancer works with clients. Pick up the phone and call. Ask how many jobs the person has given to the freelancer. Repeat business is always a good sign.

CONCLUSION: KNOW WHEN YOU NEED HELP – AND ASK FOR IT

"In the past, if you were a good writer and had a knack for people, you could build a coalition with simple messaging," said Tara Collins, an experienced non-profit communications strategist. "But you can no longer rely on writing skills alone to move the needle." Tara, and other nonprofit communicators need to understand who their supporters are, where they are, and how to reach them quickly. "Unfortunately, I can't be excellently skilled in all areas, an A-1 fighter pilot in all things communications," said Tara. "But, as a savvy practitioner with enough knowledge and understanding, I can decipher when it's in our best interest to call in experts, consultants, and third-party team members, or when to tackle that communications need in-house."

Professional development is what keeps Tara up on trends, new technology, and communications best practices so she can be more effective in her work. Expanding her personal networks and relationships by way of professional development means she can call on a colleague for an outside perspective. She can tap into an association or membership forum for vendor recommendations. She can bolster her creativity by riffing off new ideas within a learning session without fear of being torn down.

"I can't get any of that when I stay in my work bubble," said Tara. "Today's communications professionals must remain engaged and current, not just with their target communities, but also with peers and knowledge accumulation found only within conferences, webinars, coaching, associations, and book clubs."

Find the Treasure: Market Your Good Cause on a Tight Budget

Every time Walk San Francisco puts on one of their big walking events, which are fundraisers for their advocacy work, communications director Marta Lindsey tries to figure out how to get the word out to a wider audience to sell more tickets, all while spending as little money as possible. "The walks we put together are really unique and we think a lot of people would be interested, but it's hard to know how to reach them," said Marta.

"We were launching a new walk that would go around the entire perimeter of San Francisco. The event went live, and within days, it was sold out. This had never happened with one of our events," said Marta. "Sure, we'd get a surge of ticket sales right away from the people who pretty much always do all of our events, but this? Why? How? We were trying to figure it out and started asking the many people emailing us to get on a waitlist where they had heard about it."

The answer to what had worked so well? Instagram. "I admittedly spend far less time on it than I should," said Marta. She had posted the event on Instagram using the hashtag #totalsf. "In doing so, the post reached people who live in and love San Francisco, which is exactly who would be excited about walking its entire perimeter," said Marta. "Obviously, this was a huge wake-up and lesson for me in how to think about targeting and how to better harness social media – especially Instagram. And it didn't cost our organization a penny!"

In the *2019 Nonprofit Communications Trends Report*, we found that nearly half of nonprofits (45 percent) report that they do not have a set communications budget. Of those, 18 percent reported that they spend little to no money beyond salaries and 27 percent say they don't have a set budget, but find money for expenses as needed.

The half of nonprofits that do have marketing budgets typically increase those budgets as their communications team grows. For example, the median communications budget excluding salaries for a communications team of one person is between $5,000 and $20,000. That grows steadily to over $100,000 with a communications team of four or more people.

At some point in your nonprofit marketing career, you've probably found yourself in one of these three situations:

- You realized how important marketing is but didn't have the right kind of budget to support it.
- You always had a marketing program, but the budget for it just got slashed.
- You were told you needed to find ways to raise money to cover communications expenses.

All three situations can be addressed by following the strategies in this chapter, including focusing in on what's most important and forgoing the rest, taking a more friendly and casual approach to your marketing, and shifting more of your marketing online. We'll also look at where to spend and where to scrimp when money is tight.

DON'T RATTLE YOUR TIP CUP

Even when your organization is struggling, you should always keep your communications focused on your cause and the people you serve, not on your organization per se. Don't make it about you and how your agency is hurting. Make it about the good work you are trying to do, the people you are trying to serve, and how much your supporters are needed.

People want to feel like they are giving to an organization that's healthy and that makes a difference. They want to be part of your success, not your failure. If all of your messaging is about how you're having trouble paying your utility bills and how you may close your doors any minute, you'll breed more skepticism about your management abilities than confidence in your ability to make a difference. Focus on the impact your supporters can have on the people you're helping and on your cause, not on the plight of your organization.

MARKETING TRIAGE: FOCUS IN AND FORGET THE REST

When your resources are limited, you have to make choices. In Chapter 6, we discussed how you must forget the general public and focus in on the people who matter most to your success. When money is tight, it's even more important to go through the process of creating targeted groups and personas, then focus specifically on those people. You don't have the luxury of doing general outreach, public education, or awareness raising through the eyes and ears of just anyone you might happen to reach. Instead, you need to focus in – and there are several ways to get there.

The RFM model. RFM stands for *recency, frequency, and monetary value.* This is a common model in retail sales, but you can also apply it to how your list of supporters interacts with you. Recency looks at the last time a person took an action related to your organization, whether donating money, volunteering time, or opening your e-newsletter. The more recently a person took an action, the more likely that person will do it again. The same goes for frequency. How often has a supporter donated to you in the last year or how many times have they volunteered or clicked on links in your newsletter? If they frequently do any of these things, they are more likely to continue to do them. Monetary value measures the size of their gifts of money or time to you. If you need to cut back on the number of people you are communicating with, you can use the RFM model to figure out who should stay on the list and who you can put on hold. You can also use it to put certain people at the top of the list for special, personal attention.

By interests. If you are cutting back your communications budget, odds are that you are cutting back in other programmatic areas as well. Perhaps you used to operate five different programs and now you can operate only three. If your database of supporters includes information about who is interested or involved in which program, you can cut back communications with the people who were most interested in the programs you are no longer operating. In an ideal world you might try to move these people over to the other programs you continue to maintain, but if you are performing triage on your list, they are likely candidates for cutting.

Your VIPs. Every organization has a circle of Very Important People – important to your success, that is. Even if you decide that you must eliminate communications to your mailing list, you must still find a way to stay in touch with your VIPs. In addition to your major individual donors, don't overlook your grant and contract managers. Nonprofits will often overlook the program officer at the foundation or the bureaucrat at the government agency who manages the grant or contract paperwork, unless it's time to turn in a report or cash a check. Those people, however, have a lot of influence over whether you'll receive additional support in the future – and how much it will be. Be sure to keep them in the loop. Even though they represent organizational sources of money, treat these people like individual donors. Even if you eliminate your newsletter, be sure to send all of your VIPs occasional emails or personal letters updating them on your work.

Calls to action. Another way to focus in is to look at not who is on your list, but the communications you send them. Analyze the content of all of your communications; if you need to cut back on quantity to save money, make sure the remaining communications pieces focus on very clear calls to action. Know exactly why you are communicating and what you want the person on the other end to do as a result of that communication. Minimize or eliminate entirely the general "FYI" outreach. If you are always asking people to do something, you run the risk of being seen as pushy. It's nice to provide information and helpful resources to your supporters without asking for anything in return. But if the budget axe is falling, focus on calls to action that can produce results, whether it's more volunteer hours, event registrations, or donations.

GO CASUAL AND FRIENDLY

Forget the 12-page print newsletter and the 20-page annual report. Forget the fundraising gala. They are too expensive. Instead, go friendly and casual. Many of your supporters will appreciate a more relaxed approach, whether you do it for financial reasons or not!

Make phone calls and send email. Calling and emailing your supporters is much more affordable than sending them print mail. Also send personal emails – not just your e-newsletter that's sent out to everyone, but personal emails directly from you and specifically to one of your supporters. Keep both calls and emails brief and limited to one primary purpose.

Call or email to say thank you. Call or email to share a story about your work. Call or email to tell them about a fun event you think they'd enjoy, even if your group isn't the one hosting it.

This leads to the question: Do you call or email? Ideally, you know which each supporter prefers, because you've asked and are keeping track of these and other preferences.

Use these five-minute conversations to learn more about what your supporters care about, what they are interested in, and why they think your cause is so great. This is information that you need in order to cultivate that relationship long term, regardless of your financial conditions, but especially when times are tough.

Write handwritten notes. If you are cutting back on your budget, it's likely that your donors are cutting back on their personal budgets too. Which nonprofits will stay at the top of their lists? The ones with whom they feel the most personal connection.

As a board member for a local group, I was asked to write personal notes on the top of several fundraising appeal letters. At the top of a letter to a woman I knew, I wrote something like, "Hello Anne: Now that I'm serving on this board, I really see how much help our neighbors need. Thanks so much for being there for them. I'll hope you'll consider a generous gift this year, too – Kivi."

When I ran into Anne a few weeks later, she said she had a bone to pick with me. I was nervous until she said, "I had planned to stop giving to that organization because I needed to trim back this year. But when I saw your note, I had to put them back on my list." She ended with a smile and a faux-sarcastic "Thanks a lot!" Anne gave a bigger gift than she had the year before to an organization she had planned to cut off entirely. The personal touch really does work, not all of the time with everyone, but many times with enough people to make the extra effort worthwhile.

Make your events casual. Make your events more casual, personal experiences. People associate backyard barbecues and house parties with their friends, and you want to be included in that group. They associate big galas with wealth, and if you don't have money, you can't afford to throw that kind of event. When times are tough, many people don't want to be seen at lavish, over-the-top events anyway. Consumer trends show that people are craving personal, friendly, and casual experiences with people they know, like, and trust. Give your supporters what they want.

This kind of approach also translates into the auction items you request for your fundraisers. Instead of asking people to donate expensive vacations, jewelry, artwork, or other luxury items, ask them to donate special experiences instead. For example, you can ask a chef at a local restaurant to offer cooking lessons or to name a weekly special on the menu after the highest bidder.

HOW TO MAKE YOUR PRINT MARKETING MORE AFFORDABLE

Digital printing technology is changing fast, which means that printing small numbers of brochures or newsletters is much more affordable than it used to be. If you decide that you still want to send a print newsletter or other print communications using traditional offset printing, consider these steps to reduce your printing costs.

Ask your printer to recommend changes. One of the best untapped resources for lowering your print budget is your printing provider. Call up your account representative at your printer and tell him or her that you are considering dropping the newsletter entirely because of the expense of producing it (you won't be the only one). Explain that you would like to keep sending it out, but you need to make some changes to make it more affordable. Ask for suggested changes to the type of printing press, paper, format, length, inks, and so on that could bring down the price. Most printers will jump on this right away; if they don't, take copies of your current newsletter to other competitive print shops and see what they'd suggest.

Reduce the size. Paper is a large portion of your printing costs, so cutting the number of pages and reducing the size of the pages can significantly reduce your printing bill. The pieces of paper that are run through the printing press are much larger than what you end up with in your hands. Reducing the finished size of your publication by as little as a half-inch can change the way your individual pages are arranged on those bigger sheets of paper, which means you have to pay for fewer of those big sheets. Changing the size of your document can also reduce your mailing costs. If your printer is also your mail house, ask for revised mailing estimates as well.

Use thinner, off-white paper. Changing the weight of the paper (how thick it feels) and the brightness of the paper (how white it is) can sometimes reduce the cost. Even if the price difference is small, it can add up over time. Just how white does the paper need to be, especially if you are covering it mostly with text? And just how heavy should each sheet feel in your hands? The brighter the white and the heavier a sheet of paper is, the more expensive the paper will usually be. One cost-effective approach for annual reports or other larger documents is to use a heavier, more expensive paper for the cover to give the document the right look and feel, but to use a more affordable house sheet of paper for the inside.

Don't be too picky about colors. The more colors you use in traditional offset printing, the more expensive your print job will be. Even if you decide to print in full color, you can still reduce your expenses by printing strictly in a four-color process, rather than requesting full color plus specific PMS colors. Instead, convert all of your PMS colors to their CMYK equivalent. You can use the Pantone Color Bridge to see the differences in the colors using the two different processes.

In my experience, the only time this has been a real issue was when a nonprofit was working with a corporate sponsor that insisted their logo appear in certain PMS colors. Depending on the actual colors, conversion to PMS may not be a big deal, and the sponsor may be just fine with that. But if they insist on the additional PMS colors, you may want to consider asking that sponsor to cover the cost difference, if it really is a significant increase in cost.

Prepare your files correctly. The further along in the printing process that you get, the more expensive it is to make changes. Make sure your documents are proofread several times and approved by everyone who needs to see them well before you send them to the printer. Also ensure that you have prepared your digital files properly for your printer. It's not as simple as handing over the file from the computer program you used to create the document. You'll also need to supply copies of fonts and high-resolution images. Another common problem is using the wrong or mixed color profiles. (Don't know the difference between RGB and CMYK? Talk to your printer or a graphic designer before submitting your files to a printer.) When your printer has to fix any of these problems with your files, you get billed for them.

WHERE TO SPEND YOUR LIMITED DOLLARS AND WHERE TO SCRIMP

Where should you spend the marketing dollars you do have? Start with these five categories of essential expenses.

Email newsletter service provider. You can't distribute your email newsletter out of your own desktop email program for a variety of reasons. You really do need to use an email newsletter or email marketing service. Many services also include extras like built-in survey tools.

Digital cameras. Yes, you and other staff members can use your smartphones. But also consider upgrading to some dedicated cameras with better zoom functions especially for close-ups at events.

Professional design. It's important to present a professional image, yet many nonprofit websites, newsletters, and brochures look as though they were cobbled together by amateurs using the free software, templates, and imagery that every other person with a computer also owns. Hire a graphic designer to spruce up your templates or to design new ones just for you. Make it clear that you'll need to produce the actual pieces themselves, so you need a template that's easy to fill in yourself.

Professional photography. Likewise, consider hiring a professional photographer to capture the perfect images for your marketing. Great photos of real people working with your organization on its mission are incredibly valuable. Use photos on your website, in your email newsletters, and on social media. Although you can often find good options in photo-sharing sites like Flickr or through stock photography houses, it's hard to find that perfect image that says exactly what you need it to say. Explain your needs to an experienced professional photographer and you'll often be amazed at what you get back.

Professional development. Because you are implementing much if not all of your marketing program on your own, you are going to need to learn many new skills. Figure out where your biggest skill gap is and fill it with either an affordable webinar or a how-to book. If you wish you could make minor tweaks to your website design, you might need an introductory class in HTML or PHP. If you are taking and sharing lots of photos, you might want to take a Photoshop course. If you have little experience with writing for the web and email, take an online writing webinar. You'll find many affordable training courses and webinars online. The money you spend learning new skills will save you many hours of frustration and will also save your organization from having to hire freelancers or consultants to solve minor problems.

Now, what are the nonessential marketing areas in which you can scrimp? Here are the first places I would look to eliminate expenditures:

- *Advertising.* Unless you have data that proves that paid advertising works for you, don't spend money on print or online ads. Focus on search engine optimization instead and apply for a Google Grant, which gives you free search advertising credits.

- *Fancy, splashy graphics.* Focus your design resources on your overall branding, like your logo and website and newsletter templates.

- *Print mailings.* Carefully review what you are mailing out and consider cutting anything that isn't directly producing revenue and/or actions that are important to your organization (like taking advocacy actions or signing up to volunteer).

- *Donor premiums.* A handwritten thank-you letter will always be more valuable to your donors than gifts like pins, mugs, and T-shirts.

FUNDING YOUR NONPROFIT MARKETING PROGRAM

Marketing or communications programs are often the first to go in tight times, because short-sighted and highly stressed nonprofit decision makers don't consider them mission critical. Most nonprofits pay for their nonprofit marketing programs out of their unrestricted funding, which also makes them a target when mission-oriented programs are being cut.

Few foundation and government funders explicitly fund communications and marketing. Those that fund "capacity building" activities will often allow marketing and communications line items in grant proposals, especially if you clearly explain how your communications programs will help improve your organizational sustainability by building a community of loyal supporters around your cause.

You should always include communications in your programmatic, mission-oriented grant applications. As discussed throughout this book, good nonprofit marketing is really about community building. Discuss communications as a critical tactic in implementing the programmatic goal in your grant applications. You may need to describe your marketing line items in more traditional language that foundation funders are more comfortable with, such as "outreach" or "education." Corporate sponsors are more likely to understand the value of "marketing" and "communications" and to be more comfortable with that language.

CONCLUSION: ZERO COMMUNICATIONS BUDGET = ZERO SUSTAINABILITY

Your nonprofit marketing program is like a tree. It takes a long time to grow into something durable and dependable – something sustainable – that produces new supporters and keeps current ones happy year after year. Some years are better than others. Branches may break off now and then, and you need to prune away dead wood occasionally so other branches can grow stronger. You may even nip some new shoots off to direct their nutrients where they are most needed.

But never cut down the tree entirely, because once you do, it's gone. Don't cut your marketing budget entirely, even when times are tough. Prune the tree, yes, but never chop it down. Trees take far too long to grow from seeds or regenerate from stumps. If you completely ax your marketing program right now, you will feel the impact next year and for years to come. Long after your budget crunch is over, you'll still be sweating it out under the hot sun, while the other nonprofits who maintained their communications programs are sitting comfortably in the shade.

That's because nonprofit marketing is ultimately all about staying in touch with people and creating long-term relationships. When you stop talking to your friends, soon you are no longer friends. When you fail to communicate with your supporters, before long they no longer support you. Don't let this happen to your organization.

Find the Time: Get More Done in Fewer Hours

Nonprofit communications strategist Tara Collins has developed a process she calls "This Thing" to help her decide if she needs to spend some of her precious time on a project (all time is precious for all nonprofit communications pros). She asks herself these questions:

Does "this" support our mission and vision?

Does "this" need to be done?

Does "this" need to be done now?

Does "this" need to be done by me?

Who is better suited to get "this" done?

How long will "this" take to do?

Can "this" be modified to be done quicker?

You will never have enough time to do everything you want to do to market your organization and your good cause, especially if you are doing it on your own. Like any other busy professional, you need to learn some basic work-life management skills so that your email box and to-do list don't run or ruin your life. But that's not what this chapter is about. Instead, the strategies in this chapter will help you work not only faster but smarter, both strategically and tactically, on your nonprofit marketing program.

STAY CALM NOT BUSY

After working with tired, exasperated nonprofit communicators for decades and researching the differences between effective communications teams and less effective ones, I developed a model called CALM not BUSY. The model is discussed in-depth in my book, *CALM not BUSY: How to Manage Your Nonprofit's Communications for Great Results*.

207

Much of the CALM not BUSY model is related to how nonprofit communicators use their time, and we've touched on many of the specifics in earlier chapters of this book as well. Being CALM means being Collaborative, Agile, Logical, and Methodical.

C is for Collaborative. Build listening into your ongoing routine. Help others in your organization see the big picture and how their parts fit into it. Create a clear process for working together that is easy and efficient.

A is for Agile. Expect the unexpected. Have clear lines of authority, delegation, and communication internally. Create content that is agile too and easily repurposed.

L is for Logical. Integrate marketing and communications goals with programmatic and fundraising goals. Ground everything in a Quick-and-Dirty Marketing Plan. Follow best practices and experiment.

M is for Methodical. Use an editorial calendar. Set up systems and embrace tools that others can use and follow, with or without you. Find a personal productivity system that works for you.

But it's really hard to get CALM if you are still hanging on to the old ways of working, or the glorification of "busy." Nonprofit communicators constantly complain about how busy they are, and how not having enough time holds them back. I get it, trust me, I really do.

But you and I and everyone else all get the same number of hours in a day. I think it's time for a little tough love on this one, for you, for me, and for our sector as a whole.

When you give in to the idea that BUSY is normal and a legitimate way to work in this job, here's what I think you are actually embracing, especially as a nonprofit communicator:

B is for Bogus. It's bogus to think that all of that busy activity equals accomplishment. It doesn't. Focus on accomplishments not just activities (that's the same advice we offer for your annual reports!) Just because you are running all the time, reading every tweet, and attending every meeting, doesn't mean you are getting anywhere or getting anything done. Set real goals and work toward those, tracking your progress toward them, not just your general busyness.

U is for Unrealistic. We think we can get more done in less time and with fewer resources than we really can. In the nonprofit sector, this too often morphs from asking people to be resourceful to expecting miracles. Then people fall short, and we blame them personally. It's also the leading cause of martyr syndrome.

S is for Sidestepping. We – and the people we work for – avoid making the hard choices about priorities, constantly sidestepping those conversations and decisions. We want to do it all, but that's not possible, nor is it strategic. Real leaders choose.

Y is for Yoked. We are yoked, or chained, to things and habits that actually make it harder to get good work done. They constantly pull us in the wrong direction by distracting us. Chief among these are always-on devices and always pinging email and social notifications. But bad habits like meetings that, by default, always last a full hour also yoke us. Bad assumptions about ourselves and others yoke us too.

With all of this in mind, let me share a few more ways to protect the time you do have and use it more wisely.

KEEP UP WITH BEST PRACTICES, BIG BRAINS, AND COOL KIDS

I'm not fond of the term "best practices" because it implies that some great genius out there has blessed a certain way of doing things, and the rest of us don't need to bother with innovating or seeing what really works for us. But I do like what the concept stands for: that we should learn from what has worked for others, and that by doing so we'll get a head start down the right path. That's much better, especially when pressed for time, than scratching around for where to begin and fumbling around on our own. With this definition in mind, this book is full of best practices. But best practices do and should change as people collaborate and share results. Often you need to settle for something that your gut tells you will work, or something that seems good enough, rather than waiting around for the best solution possible.

With all that said, you will save a tremendous amount of time if you keep track of what others are doing and watch for successful patterns. In the nonprofit marketing world, your colleagues around the country are quite generous with sharing specific case studies at conferences and online. We are lucky to have a talented pool of bloggers both wide and deep who share great real-world advice. If you are given a new task that you don't know how to perform, a search of the nonprofit blogosphere or a question on social media will nearly always point you in the right direction.

Best practices will get you started on the right path, but to see what's around the bend, you need to pay attention to a different set of people – "big brains" and "cool kids." Big brains are the smart people not only in nonprofit marketing but also in related fields like technology, social media, and small business marketing. They have moved beyond today's conventional wisdom and are looking at how the world is changing right now so they can think through what we should all be doing tomorrow. Cool kids are nonprofit organizations, usually with either ample freedom or resources to experiment, who are not shy about sharing their experiences. It doesn't mean that everything they do is perfect—nobody and no organization is perfect. But they frequently produce great examples of best practices others can learn from. For some recommendations, go to my blog at NonprofitMarketingGuide.com and search "big brains and cool kids."

It's like an ounce of prevention for your marketing program. You'll save a tremendous amount of effort and time if you simply schedule a few minutes each day to read up on what others are talking about.

GET FEAR OUT OF THE WAY

After trying to reinvent the proverbial wheel, the next biggest time waster in the nonprofit marketing world is fear – your own fear and the fear of decision makers around you. It's frustrating to develop a new creative project or campaign only to be shut down because the decision makers just don't understand it or are too afraid to give it a shot. Many nonprofit marketing decisions, especially about content, are made out of fear. Will people be upset if we say that? Is this design too "out there" for us? Many nonprofits fall into the trap of overly conservative marketing because of fear. Try to delve into exactly what those fears are so you can address them.

To help decision makers feel more comfortable with what you are proposing, try one or more of the following methods:

- Clear up misconceptions about your target communities, which are often at the root of marketing fears, by really getting to know them.

- Share case studies from other organizations that demonstrate how what you are suggesting can be successful.

- Do a small test run of your idea first to see how it works out. Adjust accordingly.

- Hold an informal focus group on your idea, so that decision makers feel like their input has been heard.

- Develop review and approval procedures to ensure that you include in the process all the people who really do need to be included.

- Create a crisis plan to deal with the worst-case scenario, should it actually happen.

Also know that it's OK to fail. "Failing fast" is a mantra for many creative and technology professionals. We learn faster through failure. You should try lots of different things at once (but not *too* many), especially with online marketing and social media, because both the expense and the risk of colossal failure are so small, and the potential benefits are so huge. You have so much to learn through experimenting. Then share what you have learned with others and learn from what they share with you.

Hand-wringing consumes far too much time that should be spent with fingers tapping on the keyboard. Try something new, without fear. Let everyone know what you are doing, keep track of what happens, and report the results. People will be so pleasantly surprised by your refreshing transparency that they'll forget to be upset with you about the experiments that don't quite go off as you hoped.

ORGANIZE WHAT YOU'LL NEED AGAIN AND AGAIN

Every nonprofit marketer will use the same words, images, and files over and over again. Getting agreement on all of that content and then organizing it so that it can be found quickly will save you an immense amount of time.

Julia Gatten, the former communications director at AfricAid, based in Denver, Colorado, and Arusha, Tanzania, saved countless hours by building a one-pager of key messages in two formats. "It was the most useful internal document I created to build consistency and professionalism in our communications, and it led to positive feedback from staff, donors, and board members," said Julia.

By sending a series of short surveys to staff and board members in the United States and Tanzania, Julia was able to gather broad input and then eventually narrow down the organization's message to the following:

- A six-word tagline: Mentor Girls. Develop Leaders. Transform Communities.
- One short one-sentence: AfricAid mentors Tanzanian girls to become confident, educated leaders.
- One long one-sentence: AfricAid mentors secondary school girls in Tanzania to complete their education, develop into confident leaders, and transform their own lives and their communities.

They also elaborated into a three-sentence paragraph and built one-sentence descriptions for each of their programs.

In addition, the organization agreed on six personality traits for their communications work: confident, proactive, positive, powerful, professional, responsible – with definitions.

"By combining these elements in different ways, we could build out nearly any quick message we needed in seconds. Introductions to grant proposals, short phrases for thank you notes and calls, fundraising letters, event speeches, captions for social media – you name it," said Julia. "I added all the messages to a stylized page we could print out and tape to the wall above our desks. I also added the messages into a 'Quick Copy Guide' Google Doc for easy copy-and-paste access that I used nearly every week if not every day."

Every member of the staff and board had input in, access to, and training on these messages, which led to buy-in from everyone. "In situations where someone suggested leading with a different phrase, I had the power to say, 'These messages were honed and adopted by everyone as the best way to describe our work. Do they feel inaccurate to you? If so, we can revisit that process, but I am uncomfortable with making a change without comprehensive input,'" said Julia.

In addition to key phrases and descriptions like those Julia described, I also recommend that you organize the following elements.

Get Clean Copies of Your Logo in the Proper Resolutions

It seems like not a day goes by that I don't see some raggedy, blurred, or skewed nonprofit logo on TV or in print that looks like it has been sent through a fax machine three times. Don't lift your logo off your website or from a word processing document and expect it to look good elsewhere.

Go find your original artwork files. They are most likely Adobe Illustrator or Photoshop files. Once you find those, add "original" to the filename so you know not to change these source files. Then make copies and start saving them in different formats and resolutions appropriate to various uses, putting "web" and "print" in the filenames to help you keep them straight.

For online use, the resolution should be 72 ppi (pixels per inch). So, if you want your logo to appear as 1.5 inches square on your website, the dimensions would be 108 pixels by 108 pixels (that's 72 × 1.5). Save web resolution files as a .jpg, .gif, or .png. Use these on websites and blogs and in email.

For print use, the resolution should be at least 300 ppi. So, your same 1.5 square-inch logo on a piece of paper would now be 450 × 450 pixels (300 × 1.5). Save these as eps or tiff files. You can also use a .jpg, but just make sure that the resolution and size are set high enough.

For TV, I recommend sending the highest-quality logo you have and letting the company you are working with adjust the size and resolution to match their needs.

If you can't find your original artwork files, get them redrawn. Either ask your graphic designer to do it or find a volunteer or college student who knows Adobe Illustrator. You'll need to know which fonts you used or be willing to have the designer take a guess. Unless your old logo is extremely complicated, it will probably take a designer about an hour to redraw it. The $100 to $200 you spend on this will pay for itself by making your organization look much more professional.

Gather Your Boilerplate Text

Put all of those chunks of text that you use over and over in one place. That includes your mission and vision statements, plain-language descriptions of your programs, your history, your elevator speeches, staff bios, press release boilerplate, organizational Frequently Asked Questions, and anything else that you find yourself frequently copying and pasting.

Start a Style Guide

Much time is wasted correcting inconsistencies in everything from your branding, which includes how staff use your logo, colors, or fonts, to which editorial styles you prefer (anyone want to argue about serial commas?). Spare yourself and everyone else who creates content for you the misery of these arguments by creating style guides for your organization.

An editorial style sheet is a chart you fill out showing how you will use, format, and spell certain words. You can also include rules about abbreviations, capitalization, acronyms, and anything else related to how words, numbers, and punctuation appear in your publications. Include anything and everything that you end up correcting when editing someone else's work. Here are some common decisions for your style sheet.

- When do you spell out numbers? Under 10 or under 100?
- Do you use periods in acronyms or not, such as USA or U.S.A.?
- Do you hyphenate certain words? For example, is it email or e-mail? Decision-maker or decision maker?
- Formatting phone numbers – use parentheses around the area code or not? Periods or hyphens in between segments?
- Formatting email addresses – all lower case, or are capital letters OK?
- Formatting website addresses – include the http:// and www. or not?

You should also create design style sheets that specify which fonts, colors, and other design elements you use, and when and where you use them.

Distribute your style guides widely and put them in places staff and volunteers can easily access, such as an electronic copy on your intranet or printed copies on an office bulletin board. Supplement the style guide with a running list of examples or answers to style questions raised by staff.

CONCLUSION: GIVE YOURSELF A BREAK

When I'm stuck on a problem, I do one of three things: take a walk, take a shower, or take a nap. Nearly every time, by physically removing myself from the problem and giving my brain a break, I find a creative solution.

I'm not alone. Neuroscientists who study how the human brain solves problems say that our ability to find those creative insights is related to whether we can find connections between seemingly disparate pieces.[1] Time away from a problem is a key element in finding those connections. Studies show that creative revelations often arise when our minds are busy with some unrelated task. Sleeping on a problem increases the likelihood that you'll solve it.

In the chaos of your daily life as a nonprofit marketer, remember that you'll actually be more creative – and therefore often more efficient – if you stop spending so much time focusing on a problem and give yourself a break.

Conclusion: How Do You Know Whether You Are Doing a Good Job?

chapter
EIGHTEEN

Nonprofit marketing is, without question, a growing field. But it's still very much a young field too, especially if you take some of the concepts I've presented in this book to heart, such as becoming your own media mogul and thinking of yourself as a community organizer. There is no single job description for a nonprofit marketer. I'm not even sure we'd have it covered if we came up with 10 different job descriptions.

Although there's a lot of fun to be had working in such a diverse field with so much pioneering going on right before our eyes, that also means it can be tough to gauge how well you are doing. Are you any good at this? If you really want to measure your success, you have to cobble together a performance review that matches your cobbled-together – and frequently changing – job description.

It's relatively easy to measure the effectiveness of many of the specific tactics that you will use in marketing; it's harder, but possible, to measure yourself against many of the objectives we reviewed in Part One.

But what about those really big changes we are seeking when we market our good causes? You market your organization and its programs and services, but to what end?

As you sit back and look at your nonprofit marketing program as a whole and evaluate your own performance as a nonprofit marketer, consider these questions:

- *Does your marketing strategy make you stand out from the crowd?* Are you conveying what is unique and valuable about your organization and programs? Is it clear to the people who matter most to your success who you are and what

215

you do? Is your marketing different enough from that of other organizations working in the same space?

- *Is your organization perceived as a leader or an expert?* What's your status or reputation within your field? How does your marketing strategy help you position yourself or your nonprofit as a leader or expert? How trusted is your organization, and how does your marketing plan maintain and build trust with your supporters?

- *Do your current supporters remember who you are?* You might be surprised how many donors forget that they've made gifts to a nonprofit organization. After all, why would they remember, if the nonprofit doesn't work on maintaining those open lines of communication? Are you keeping those good feelings you worked to create through your initial outreach going strong? Are you communicating regularly with supporters? Are you reminding them what you do?

- *Do your current supporters think of you favorably?* Does your strategy include multiple ways to foster good feelings about your cause and your organization among your supporters? Or are your supporters feeling overlooked, forgotten, or used? Are you repeatedly thanking them for their support? Are you explaining the results you created using their last gift of time, money, or talent? Are you sharing stories with them about why they matter so much to your success? Do you make your supporters, especially your biggest fans, feel like part of your team?

- *Are you connecting with new people?* Unless your target community is a very well-defined and limited group of people without much turnover, your marketing programs should be bringing new people into your community of participants and supporters. This will often require trying entirely new approaches to tap into those networks where you don't have a presence now. Have you identified who your newest supporters will be? Are you listening to them and learning what's important to them?

- Perhaps most important, *do you love your job?*

Think about each of these questions. If you can answer a resounding "Yes!" then give yourself a pat on the back and share the secrets of your success with other colleagues. If you answer "No" or you simply aren't sure, sketch out a plan to get closer to "Yes!" in the coming weeks, months, and years.

Your nonprofit marketing work is about making the world a better place. It's important. It matters. You can do it. Thank you for taking it on.

NOTES

Chapter 2: Defining Marketing in the Nonprofit Sector

1. Thomas L. Friedman, "The Power of Green," *The New York; Times Magazine*, April 15, 2007. See https://www.nytimes.com/2007/04/15/magazine/15green.t.html

Chapter 3: Nonprofit Marketing Plans in Theory – and in the Real World

1. Kivi Leroux Miller, "The Making of 'Do More Than Cross Your Fingers,'" Kivi's Nonprofit Communications Blog, September 2, 2009. See http://www.nonprofitmarketingguide.com/blog/2009/09/02/the-making-of-do-more-than-cross-your-fingers/

Chapter 6: Define Your Community: Who Do You Want to Reach?

1. Based in part on "The Great Schlep: Who Says Alienating Whole Segments of the Giving Public Is Always a Bad Thing?" by Sarah Durham, *Fundraising Success*, March 1, 2009. See http://www.fundraisingsuccessmag.com/article/the-great-schlep-403794_1.html

Chapter 7: Create a Powerful Message: What Do You Want to Say?

1. "Save the Darfur Puppy," Nicholas Kristof, *New York; Times*, May 10, 2007. See http://select.nytimes.com/2007/05/10/opinion/10kristof.html

2. "'If I Look at the Mass I Will Never Act': Psychic Numbing and Genocide," Paul Slovic, Decision Research and University of Oregon, in *Judgment and Decision Making*, April 2007, 2(2), 79–95. See http://journal.sjdm.org/7303a/jdm7303a.htm

3. For more on the power of the heart over the head, see the following:

"When It's Head Versus Heart, The Heart Wins," *Newsweek*, February 11, 2008. "Emotional Ads Work Best," http://www.neurosciencemarketing .com/blog/articles/emotional-ads-work-best.htm; "Nonprofit Marketing: The Power of Personalization," http://www.neurosciencemarketing.com/ blog/articles/nonprofit-marketing-personal.htm

4. "Anatomy of a Direct Mail Makeover at UC Berkeley," Kivi Leroux Miller. See http://www.nonprofitmarketingguide.com/resources/fundraising/ anatomy-of-a-direct-mail-makeover-at-uc-berkeley

5. For additional information on using reason and statistics in marketing, see the following: "The Storytelling Power of Numbers," http://www. frameworksinstitute.org/ezine25.html; "Making Numbers Count," http://www.sightline.org/research/sust_toolkit/ communications-strategy/ flashcard5-landing-NUMBERS

6. "The Real Darfur Puppy," Nicholas Kristof, *New York; Times*, May 10, 2007. See http://kristof.blogs.nytimes.com/2007/05/10/the-real-darfur-puppy/

Chapter 8: Spread Your Message Further by Telling Great Stories

1. Richard Maxwell and Robert Dickman, *The Elements of Persuasion* (New York: Harper, 2007): p. 5.

Chapter 9: Adopt an Attitude of Gratitude

1. Jen Shang, Adrian Sargeant, Kathryn Carpenter, and Harriet Day, *Learning to Say Thank You: The Role of Donor Acknowledgements*, The Institute for Sustainable Philanthropy website (Sept 2018). See https:// philanthropy-centre.org/wp-content/uploads/2018/11/Learning-to-Say-Thank-You-eBook.pdf

Chapter 12: Become an Expert Source for the Media and Decision Makers

1. Peter Panepento and Antionette Kerr, *Modern Media Relations for Non-profits: Creating an Effective PR Strategy for Today's World* (Lexington, NC: Bold & Bright Media, 2018).

2. Antionette Kerr, "Newsjacking: From Roadkill to Rock Stars," Kivi's Nonprofit Communications Blog, June 12, 2019. See https://www.nonprofit marketingguide.com/blog/2019/06/12/newsjacking-from-roadkill-to-rock-stars/

Chapter 13: Build Engagement: Stay in Touch and Keep the Conversation Going

1. Penelope Burk, *Donor-Centered Fundraising* (Chicago: Cygnus Applied Research, 2003), p. 19.

2. Karen Hopper, "2018 EOY Fundraising: The Good, the Bad, and the Meh," Jan 29, 2019. See https://www.mrss.com/lab/2018-eoy-fundraising-the-good-the-bad-and-the-meh/

Chapter 14: Empower Your Fans to Build More Support

1. "Participation Inequality: Encouraging More Users to Contribute," Jakob Nielsen's Alertbox, October 9, 2006. See http://www.useit.com/alertbox/participation_inequality.html

2. "What Is WOM Marketing?" Word of Mouth Marketing Association. See http://womma.org/wom101/

Chapter 17: Find the Time: Get More Done in Fewer Hours

1. "Break Through by Taking Breaks," Matthew E. May, American Express OPEN Forum, September 17, 2009. See http://www.openforum.com/idea-hub/topics/the-world/article/break-through-by-taking-breaks-matthew-e-may

.com, .net, .org The extension of a website address or domain name. Also called the top level domain (TLD). Originally .com was reserved for commercial sites, .net for Internet service providers, and .org for nonprofit organizations. Now anyone can purchase and use any of these TLDs. I recommend that you purchase all three for your websites.

ALT text for photos "Alternate text" used to summarize what's in an image when the image can't be viewed on a website or in an email. Assists the visually impaired who use screen readers and is also seen when images are blocked in an email.

analytics Statistics generated about visitors to a website or readers of an email. Analytics can help track which pages visitors look at, what links they click on, and how they found the site.

anchor text The text on a website or in an email that, when clicked, takes you to another place on that page or on the internet. Anchor text is usually underlined. Also called *link text* or *hypertext link*.

blog A "web log" or online journal that is frequently updated, with the most recent updates appearing at the top of the page, in reverse chronological order.

blogosphere The collective community created by all of the blogs on a topic; the portion of the World Wide Web made up of blogs.

bouncing emails An email that is not received and is returned to the sender. A hard bounce occurs when a message is returned because the address was invalid. A soft bounce occurs when an email is returned due to a full inbox or other technical problems, even though the email address is valid.

CAN-SPAM The Controlling the Assault of Non-Solicited Pornography and Marketing Act of 2003, which established rules regarding the sending of bulk email, such as requiring an "unsubscribe" option and outlawing misleading subjects and deceptive return addresses.

click-through rate The percentage of email recipients who click on a link in a particular email message.

domain name The primary part of your website address; for examples, the domain name of http://www.nonprofitmarketingguide.com is nonprofitmarketingguide.com.

domain registrar A company that manages the registration of internet domain names. Your domain registrar and web host may or may not be the same company.

downloads A file, such as a PDF, video, or audio file, that a user can transfer from a website to a personal computer. Some downloads are free; others you must pay for before being given access to the file.

Google Analytics A free program by Google for tracking website statistics.

Google Grant Program by Google that allows nonprofits to participate in Google Ads for free. The nonprofit can place advertising on search engine results pages and throughout Google's advertising network.

Google Trends A tool for comparing search volume patterns for specific keywords across particular regions, categories, and time frames. The advanced version, Google Insights, provides additional analysis.

HTML Hyper Text Markup Language. It is made up of various codes enclosed by angle brackets < >. Web browsers (like Chrome or Firefox) read HTML and then display it as web pages. The same code is used to create HTML emails (emails with colors, fonts, images, and so on).

keywords The specific terms (single words and phrases) used by someone searching for something on the internet. By knowing the keywords that best describe your organization and its work, you can track mentions of those keywords on the internet. You can also use those words on your own website, so that search engines will associate your website with those topics.

long-tail, long-tail keywords   Typically, phrases with three or more words that are much more specific versions of your keywords. For example, if one of your keywords is "homeless shelter," examples of long-tail keywords are "homeless shelter for families" and "homeless shelter New York City."

microsites   Mini-websites, with their own domain names, that are often created for specific campaigns. They can be independent websites or part of a larger site.

open rate   The percentage of email recipients who open the email message. Can be measured only for HTML emails.

opt-out   Request by a recipient of an email newsletter to be removed from your email list. The recipient opts out by unsubscribing.

permalink   A direct link to a specific blog post or forum entry.

permission-based email marketing   Practice in which emails are sent only to those who have requested information or given permission to receive emails from a particular organization.

redirect   Action taken when a user types in one website address and is automatically taken to another website address. For example, you can redirect someone who types "yoursite.com" to "yoursite.org" if you own both domain names and your main site has the .org extension.

retweet   Forwarding someone else's tweet (an update on Twitter) to your own Twitter followers.

RSS   Real Simple Syndication, a way for websites that are updated frequently, such as blogs or news sites, to send new content automatically to subscribers. Readers of these types of sites subscribe and then receive updates to an RSS reader, instead of having to check all the different sites all the time.

RSS reader   A software tool used to collect, manage, and read content delivered via RSS feeds. For example, you can use an RSS reader to subscribe to blogs and to read the new content published on those blogs, without having to revisit the blog's home page.

search engine   Online tool used to locate information on the internet. Google, Yahoo!, and Bing are search engines.

search engine optimization   Action taken to improve the effectiveness of your website so that search engines rank it higher on their search engine results pages when people search on your keywords.

search engine rankings The order in which results of a web search are listed. The most relevant websites should appear toward the top of the list. Sites are ranked according to a complex formula that includes how keywords are used on the site and how many other related websites link to the site.

social media Online sites and tools that allow people to easily create, share, and discuss content, including articles, images, and video. Includes image- and video-sharing sites and social networking sites.

stock photography Photos that can be purchased or licensed as opposed to hiring a photographer to produce new ones.

tags Descriptive keywords used to categorize an article, such as a blog entry or a web page a user wishes to save and share through a social bookmarking site. Tagging can help the entry be found more easily by search engines.

tweet An update sent out on Twitter.

unsubscribe The act of removing oneself from an email list. Can usually be done by following the "unsubscribe" link in legitimate email, but users should be cautious about using any link in an uninvited email.

URL Uniform Resource Locator, a web page's address. http://www.nonprofitmarketingguide.com is a URL.

web hosting Storage of your website pages on a computer server owned by the hosting company. The web host then makes the pages available to internet users. Your web host and your domain registrar may or may not be the same company.

ACKNOWLEDGMENTS

As I drafted this new edition of *The Nonprofit Marketing Guide*, it was important to me to add more real-life examples to better illustrate the advice on these pages. Throughout this book, you'll find several examples that also appeared in the first edition. My thanks again, a decade later, to those who shared such timeless stories with me.

But you'll also read many new personal accounts shared by nonprofit communications professionals specifically for this second edition. Many of these storytellers read the first edition of this book and were eager to be a part of the second edition. They too wanted to share what they have learned themselves over the last decade.

My heartfelt thanks to each of these new story contributors, in the order in which their stories first appear.

Jane Austin

Jeanette Stokes

Tara Collins

Melissa Cipollone

Courtney Kassel

Beth Hallowell

Cheryl Megurdichian

Bridget Bestor

Christina Hill

Kelly Nutty

Hillary Ryan

Heidi Gollub

Amy Souers Kober

Neely Conway

Amy Cranch

Corinna Wagner

Tiffany Nyklickova

Marta Lindsey

Julia Gatten

THE AUTHOR

Kivi Leroux Miller is the founder and CEO of Nonprofit Marketing Guide, where she helps nonprofit communications professionals learn their jobs and love their jobs through a variety of training and coaching programs.

She has personally mentored hundreds of nonprofit communications directors and communications teams as a certified executive coach. Kivi is also a frequent keynote, workshop, and webinar presenter and the award-winning author of three books and a popular blog.

INDEX

Page references followed by *fig* indicate an illustrated figure; followed by *t* indicate a table.

Influencer (or ambassador) marketing, 20
Influencers (PSI or participants, supporters, influencers), 64
   See also Participants
Informal focus groups, 51–53
Instagram
   Cal Grad Day promoted on, 171
   changing the way we connect, 120
   performing keyword or hashtag searches on, 55–56
   See also Social media
Instagram Stories, 167
Instant messaging, 25
Institute of Practitioners in Advertising, 80
Intelligence gathering. *See* Listening strategies
Interaction, 16
Internet & American Life Project, 55
Interplast, 96–97
Irrelevant stories, 101

J

Jessica's persona, 73, 123, 124
Jewish Council for Education and Research (JCER), 65–66
JewsVote.org, 65
John's persona, 73, 123, 124

K

Kassel, Courtney, 41
Kerr, Antionette, 155, 156
Keyword searches, 55–56
King, Basil, 9
Knowledge
   listening to expand your professional, 58
   marketing objective related to, 22–23
   See also Educational activities
Kober, Amy Souers, 143–144
KPIs (Key Performance Indicators), 24
Kristina's gratitude story, 105–106
Kristof, Nicholas, 78, 88–89

L

Language issues
   emotional words, 100–101
   "general public" misnomer, 5, 64, 68
   learning the field and community lingo, 58
   passionate communications instead of wonky jargon, 164–165
   Second Sense's renaming process, 63
   what to call your targeted community, 63
Leaders. *See* Nonprofit leaders
Liberty Hill Foundation, 41

Lifestyle writing, 117
Lindsey, Marta, 197
LinkedIn, 120
Listening benefits
   "Bingo!" moment, 146–147
   build your network/connect with your community, 56
   create better content, 57
   encourage more engagement on your issues, 57–58
   expand your personal knowledge and capacity, 58
   never stop listening to achieve, 59
Listening networks
   conduct online surveys, 53
   connecting with your community and building your, 56
   description of an effective, 50
   formal focus groups, 50–51
   informal focus groups, 51–53
Listening strategies
   analyze your website, email, and social media, 54–55
   Beth Hallowell on benefits of, 49
   how to watch and listen, 50–51
   performing keyword or hashtag searches, 55–56
   review media kits and advertising, 55
   watching relevant polling and survey data, 55
Location-based marketing, 21
Logic, reason, and statistics, 83–84
Logo copies, 212–213
Loyalty (donor), 22

M

Made to Stick (Heath and Heath), 92, 93
Maher, Katherine, 105
Maintenance stage, 67t
Marathon Kids, 131–132
Marketing
   differentiating between communication and, 14–15
   as essential to fundraising, 8
   the official definition of, 12, 13
   See also Nonprofit marketing
Marketing effectiveness realities
   1. effectiveness depends on skilled professional, 3–4
   2. need for supportive organizational culture, 4
   3. there will always be too much to do, 4
   4. there is no such thing as a general public, 5
   5. you need to manage your own media empire, 5–6